Intelligence Requirements for the 1980's:

Elements of Intelligence

Revised Edition

Consortium for the
Study of Intelligence

Intelligence Requirements for the 1980's:

Elements of Intelligence

Revised Edition

Edited by:
Roy Godson

Published by
National Strategy
Information Center, Inc.

Distributed by

Transaction Books
New Brunswick (USA) and London (UK)

Intelligence Requirements for the 1980's:
Elements of Intelligence
REVISED EDITION
First Printing

Published by
National Strategy Information Center, Inc.
1730 Rhode Island Avenue, N.W.
Washington, D.C. 20036

Printed in the United States of America

Table of Contents

Elements
of
Intelligence

An Introduction
to the
Revised Edition

Roy Godson

In the 1970's, in the US, an unprecedented public debate was initiated about the role of foreign intelligence in an open society. The debate has been of long duration; indeed, it is far from over. Heightened by congressional inquiries and intensive media coverage, the issues initially centered almost exclusively on one facet of the subject—the real and alleged abuses, and particularly violations of American civil liberties, by the intelligence agencies. Given the primary function of US national security policy—to protect and enhance the values of our society—it is clearly important that intelligence activities not diminish or otherwise adversely affect those values.

Some serious abuses were uncovered by the investigations of the 1970's, and corrective measures were implemented to prevent their recurrence. The debate served a useful purpose.

Unfortunately, it did not go far enough. Little or no attention was given to another major aspect of intelligence in a free society—the quality of our intelligence system. Was it capable of defending our open society successfully? Was its record to date a mere chronicle of failure, or could we point to successes as well? Answers to those questions were obscured by the rhetoric of criticism and sensational exposure. So, too, other instances of civil liberties violation, some on a very large scale, aroused no adverse reaction at all—as for example, Soviet intercepts of hundreds of thousands of American telephonic communications each year, brought to public attention by Senator Moynihan but otherwise generally ignored.

Systematic consideration of foreign intelligence and the values of an open society requires scrutiny of all these issues. Success stories are understandably hard to come by, and they rarely make as good copy as failures. Thus a reading of the congressional investigation reports would leave the impression that US covert action was either entirely immoral (promoting assassinations and interfering unilaterally in democratic politics of other countries) or of no utility. Intelligence analysis and estimates fared little better. The Pike Committee found only inadequacy; the Church Committee ignored the subject almost entirely.

A truly balanced inquiry and attendant public discussion at that time would have placed us in a better position to address major issues that remain important, even vital, today. Fortunately, the thrust of public scrutiny has moved on to these issues. Concern is now focused on existing intelligence capabilities matched against present and future needs. How good are we today? Will our system be able to meet the challenge of the 1980's? What are our needs likely to be? These are important questions, and many of their aspects can be aired effectively and properly in open session.

Consortium for the Study of Intelligence

With these considerations in mind, a group of scholars interested in national security policy, law, and values of the open society, came together in early 1979 under the auspices of the *National Strategy Information Center*. Their purpose was to study intelligence, and to determine what steps might be taken to ensure that US performance would enhance American values. To achieve their objectives, the group, calling itself the *Consortium for the Study of Intelligence,* planned to assemble scholars, intelligence specialists, and other organizations and individuals interested in the subject. Papers were to be commissioned from specialists in various areas, and discussed in a series of meetings over a four-year period. The results of their deliberations were to be published and made available to concerned governmental and nongovernmental entities, and to academics teaching intelligence in the context of diplomacy and foreign operations.

The first meeting of the Consortium took place on April 27 and 28, 1979, in Washington, D.C., and was devoted to an overall examination of US needs respecting the four major elements of intelligence—analysis and estimates, clandestine collection, counterintelligence, and covert action. It was followed at intervals by successive colloquia devoted to each of the major elements of intelligence. The proceedings from the five meetings, encompassing the papers submitted on each occasion and the exchanges of views among the fifty to sixty scholars, former and current US intelligence officials, congressional staff specialists in intelligence, members of the Consortium, and others present, have been published in five volumes under the title, *Intelligence Requirements for the 1980's.* The first of these, subtitled *Elements of Intelligence,* is offered here in revised format and updated against the backdrop of changes in the legal and political scene postdating its original publication.

Elements of Intelligence became in effect an introduction to the four succeeding volumes of the series. Many of the problems and issues dealt with in the latter are posed initially in *Elements*. During the more than three years that have elapsed since its original printing, *Elements* has gone through three printings and has come into wide use as a primer or introduction for persons newly addressing the subject of intelligence. The book, however, does not start at the beginning. Its chapters launch full-blown into the realm of intelligence, with only a passing nod on the part of the writers in the direction of definitions. A student or general reader is thus called upon to acknowledge premises that could profit by more discursive treatment than they are given.

What, for example, is intelligence? The meaning of the word varies among peoples and even within governments. Western states contrast sharply with most non-Western and totalitarian states in the way they view and apply it. The latter generally direct their intelligence systems first against their own societies and only then against external objectives. They are free to employ methods proscribed in western democracies, and they have few limitations on the way intelligence can be used. Whereas during wartime in western democracies intelligence enjoys high prestige and government support, the advent of peace generally results in curtailment of authority and reduced commitment of resources. Totalitarian states appear immune to such fluctuations. Ruling communist parties in particular see little distinction between war and peace, and their intelligence and security establishments remain very powerful at all times.

In the American context intelligence connotes information needed or desired by the Government in pursuance of its national interests. It includes the process of obtaining, evaluating, protecting, and eventually exploiting the same information. But that is not all. Intelligence encompasses the defense of US institutions from penetration and harm by hostile intelligence services. The term is also used to describe the mechanism or mechanisms and the bureaucracy which accomplish these activities. Hence, US intelligence, or the intelligence community. Intelligence is at once knowledge, organization, and process. Its four major disciplines (analysis, collection, counterintelligence, covert action) are interdependent. Success in any one of the four is related to the level of effectiveness achieved in the others.

Intelligence collection, however skillfully pursued, needs the protection of counterintelligence lest its mechanisms be penetrated and its analytic product distorted. Covert action can never succeed unless it is based on sound intelligence, and it too needs the support of effective counterintelligence to ensure the authenticity and security of its assets. Counterintelligence protects the other disciplines. Sustained interaction among the practitioners of each is vital to the mutual understanding and cooperation that must characterize an effective intelligence system. In organizational terms, this means that collection and analysis, counterintelligence and covert action are not completely separable. As elements of the same craft, they form part of a whole.

Clandestine Collection

As it is used in these volumes, the term *clandestine collection* denotes the key element, the *sine qua non*, of the intelligence process—namely, the acquisition of valued information or data, which as a rule are not readily available from open sources. Both human and technological methods may be employed. They are designed to breach or surmount the barriers that stand in the way of that sought-after knowledge. The resources of publicly available, openly accessible information must first be probed and exploited as an essential backdrop and foundation upon which the former can be evaluated.

If the information is highly protected within a government or society, it may be obtainable only through specialized and often devious methods—i.e., espionage, or by technical means. In other instances restricted information may be attainable through elicitation or even through direct solicitation. Thus diplomats and military attaches develop and exploit their foreign contacts actively and often aggressively toward this end.

Technical collection, with its myriad sub-disciplines in the signals and imagery fields, has expanded so enormously since World War II, and is now producing such vast quantities of information that some believe human source collection can now be dispensed with. This appears to be unrealistic. Human sources provide major, frequently indispensable, insights into intentions and the nuances of decision making that facilitate understanding of a country, its leaders, and the issues they may be grappling with.

Analysis and Estimates

Raw intelligence, whether acquired through human, technical or open sources must be collated, scrutinized, and processed carefully. The aim of this analytic process is a finished product more intelligible and usable than the data and information drawn upon to prepare it. Exploiting all available material, analysis strives for clarity while screening out error, non-essentials, and possible deception.

The types of analysis produced by the American intelligence community vary from current reports on subjects of immediate interest to periodic studies on questions of longer-term concern. The first category would include CIA's National Intelligence Daily and the Defense Intelligence Daily, plus the daily briefs prepared specifically for the President. All are short and descriptive. They are keyed to important issues of the day, and use information from sensitive and open sources. CIA, the Defense Intelligence Agency, and the State Department also produce studies that examine issues in greater depth. Their topics may derive from expressed interests of consumers at the policymaking level, or from a program of priorities generated within the Agency. The views of senior analysts on what is significant may likewise result in a specific analysis.

An important distinction must be made in these longer studies between those which reflect solely CIA opinion and others which have been coordinated among the components of the intelligence community. The National Intelligence Estimates (NIEs) are the most important in the latter category; they may appear annually, or less frequently. Special NIEs are produced *ad hoc,* generally in response to heightened interest at the policy level of government on particular issues or problems. All of these coordinated products are considered in theory to represent a consensus in the intelligence community, with dissent recorded in footnotes, but in their final form they reflect the position of the Director of Central Intelligence.

Counterintelligence

This most controversial element of the intelligence system does not lend itself to ready definition. Stripped to its bare essentials, counterintelligence can be described as the identification, neutralization and, under certain conditions, manipulation of other countries' intelligence services. It aims first to safeguard information a government deems sensitive and does not wish to reach the hands of its adversaries—or, possibly, even its friends. It aims further at protecting government and its various components from penetration and manipulation by their foreign counterparts.

There are both active and passive aspects in these undertakings, although the lines of distinction between them are hazy. There is a choice between waiting passively for the adversary service to move, or taking forthright action to find his agents, thwart and, if feasible, gain control over them. That accomplished, it may be possible to manipulate the other service to serve a variety of purposes. A classic example of aggressive counterintelligence is the "double-cross" system of manipulated human intelligence during World War II.

Manipulation of an opposing intelligence service may sometimes be effected through deception in the form of information, passed via human or technical channels, designed to convey specific impressions, or misimpressions, to the recipient. Like other counterintelligence measures, it too is subject to defensive efforts by the target country or service. The sensitivity attaching to all facets of the discipline in a democracy is obviously very great. Sometimes it may be necessary to investigate the activities of possibly innocent American citizens in order to identify and counter the activities of hostile intelligence services. The strong reaction against this position on the part of some congressional leaders and the press in the mid-1970's reflects the latent mistrust that has clouded the subject since the American Revolution. In the 1970's it resulted in restrictive laws, executive orders, and internal agency guidelines, which now are slowly being changed.

Covert Action

This element of intelligence involves, in strictly American parlance, the clandestine effort to influence the internal—and often external—affairs of a foreign country. It is an adjunct to diplomacy, which also seeks to influence political conditions and events abroad. The US has used it from time to time since 1775 as an instrument in foreign operations.

A distinguishing feature of such attempts to influence events in a foreign country is that their actual sponsorship and linkage to external sources is concealed. This is often difficult, especially when the activity grows large and complex.

Political, propaganda, and paramilitary activity command the great bulk of covert action effort. Some of it may be applied discretely, as in the case of political guidance, advice, counsel, or financial assistance to individual leaders or political figures. Or, it may entail support on a larger scale to political parties and to a variety of private organizations which are politically important. Propaganda programs may be targetted at the country as a whole, with the intent to affect overall opinions and attitudes. They may also be conducted on a smaller scale, via selected media or channels, aimed at influencing specific elements of the population. In special circumstances economic action may be undertaken covertly, although this is understood to be comparatively rare. Finally, there is paramilitary activity, perhaps the most difficult—and controversial—form of covert action. Military operations, obviously, do not lend themselves toward concealment.

The objectives of all categories of covert action must be consonant with overall policies and goals, and it is imperative that the action be coordinated effectively and on a sustained basis at senior echelons of the government. Without a consensus encompassing objectives and the main contours of *modus operandi*, a given operation faces an almost certain prospect of failure and, in the US these days, exposure.

* * * * * * * * * *

The five essays presented at the April 1979 meeting of the Consortium and reprinted here after some revision were intended to be provocative, to identify issues, problems, and to suggest areas meriting scrutiny at future meetings of the Consortium. Those purposes seem to have been well served. Although significant differences emerged among the paper writers, and between the later and various participants, there was general agreement that all the elements of intelligence are important, that they are symbiotically related, and that the US should move to strengthen and improve its capabilities in the four major areas of intelligence activity.

(1) Most participants believed there was much room for improvement in the area of analysis and estimates. They concluded that past performance in the evaluation of collected data had been inadequate.

(2) The need for improving clandestine activities was stressed. Although espionage, counterintelligence, and covert action pose special problems for a free society, these functions were considered essential if such a society is to remain free and achieve its objectives in world affairs.

(3) The former intelligence professionals also stressed that if the US is to have an adequate capability in the future, several steps needed to be taken immediately. The lead time in the development of intelligence capabilities can sometimes equal and even exceed that in the deployment of strategic weapons. This is especially true for clandestine activities. Following the exposures and intensive publicity of the early and middle 1970's, it was apparent that US capabilities had been reduced significantly. By failing to reverse that trend and rebuild needed assets, the US, by the 1980's, would find itself unable to exercise certain critical intelligence options.

(4) The participants agreed that while revised legislative charters might be beneficial for the intelligence community, some of the legal arrangements then being discussed would actually detract from US security. In particular, it was agreed that many of the foreign intelligence guidelines embodied in the Carter Administration's Executive Order 12036 had already harmed the intelligence mission, and would be worse if they passed into law. (E.O. 12036 has since been replaced by E.O. 12333, obviating some, but by no means all of those concerns. Ed.)

(5) Two other pieces of legislation also were critized—the Hughes-Ryan Amendment to the Foreign Assistance Act of 1974, and some aspects of the Freedom of Information Act. There was general agreement that while the objectives of this legislation were laudable, in practice their implementation had damaged US capabilities, and that there were better ways of achieving the intended objectives. It was argued that the Hughes-Ryan Amendment, which requires the President personally to approve of covert actions and to report to eight committees of congress, had effectively ruled out major covert action as an option. The Freedom of Information Act, it was argued, was so loosely written that it has had the effect of damaging US ability to collect valuable positive intelligence as well as counterintelligence. (The Hughes-Ryan Amendment was subsequently

rescinded in part by the Intelligence Authorization Act of 1981 [P.L. 96-450]. Reporting on presidential approval of covert action operations was in effect reduced from eight committees to two—the House and Senate Intelligence Committees. A presidential finding, however, and prior notification to Congress are still required. The two committees are to be kept fully and currently informed of all significant intelligence activities, including "intelligence failures." The Freedom of Information Act, however, remains in effect notwithstanding lengthy hearings and the tabling of numerous proposals aimed at changing it. Ed.)

(6) There were differences of opinion among the former intelligence professionals and among some of the participants about the need to reorganize the intelligence community—a subject receiving a fair amount of media attention at that time. Some participants suggested that if there were to be a substantial improvement in US capabilities, a continuation of past organizational arrangements, as broadly set out in the National Security Act of 1947 and its amendments of 1949, was insufficient for the purpose. They maintained that a major reorganization was a necessary first step toward achieving improvements. In principle, legislative charters for the agencies might be a good starting point.

(7) There was general agreement that more attention should be devoted to future US needs in each major area of intelligence activity. It was suggested that subsequent meetings of the Consortium focus on analysis and estimates, counterintelligence, covert action, and clandestine collection. (This was accomplished in 1980-1982, and the results are available in the *Intelligence Requirements* series, Volumes II-V. Ed.)

The individual essays that follow should be read in the context of the foregoing. They represent in effect the first stage of an extended study of the elements of intelligence in general, and in particular of the future requirements of the US intelligence system.

The chapter on *Analysis and Estimates, Quality in U.S. Intelligence*, was written by Lt. General Daniel O. Graham, US Army (Ret.). General Graham has had extensive experience in the intelligence community. For many years he served as a senior official in Army intelligence, and in the Defense Intelligence Agency (DIA). In

1974 he was appointed Deputy Director of Central Intelligence for the Intelligence Community, and then in 1974 he became Director of DIA. After retiring from DIA in 1976, General Graham served on Team B which was established by then Director of Central Intelligence George Bush to engage in a competitive analysis of the Soviet strategic arms buildup.

General Graham supports the concept of competitive analysis. He maintains that US estimates have not been accurate and policymakers have not received adequate intelligence, in large part because alternative views have not reached them. His major thesis is that the creation of competitive, centralized, analytic agencies would produce better intelligence to further this end, he would separate the functions of the Director of Central Intelligence as overseer of the intelligence community from those he discharges Director of CIA.

In the discussion following General Graham's presentation, his views were contested by certain participants, and supported by others. Competitive analysis received generally favorable treatment, although the point was made that the total volume of available intelligence data was too great to permit it in every case. Others held that policymakers should recognize that some issues or questions, on the basis of available evidence, simply do not warrant single or final conclusions. Considerable emphasis was put on the importance of open sources of information as a foundation for subsequent analysis and estimates based on clandestinely collected data.

A widened role for outside experts in the analytic process also received favorable comment as a way to encourage the airing and utilization of diverse points of view. Still others contested General Graham's negative assessment of the quality of intelligence estimates over the years, arguing that while there had indeed been failures—some of them notable, the overall record is much better than suggested and the errors perhaps less egregious than described.

Not all agreed that the failures cited were avoidable. Reasonable men, after all, may reach quite different conclusions after studying the same body of evidence. Note was made of the real problems entailed in reaching a consensus on an intelligence issue. This usually means that someone has to compromise—no easy task when connections are strongly held on both sides. And at the receiving end are the policymakers—often busy, harassed, strong-minded men who develop, or already have, some expertise of their own. It is not to be assumed that they will sit back passively as detached consumers of information. They may argue, complain, or raise a storm about an analysis they cannot swallow—and not necessarily on "political" grounds. Or, faced with the product of competitive analysis, is the policymaker certain to be able to fight his way through volumes of data and conflicting commentary. His alternatives include ignoring it, or calling in his own "expert."

General Graham's position is reiterated in the current edition. During the passage of time since the first printing, the structure of the US intelligence community has undergone some slight modification, but in General Graham's opinion the basic problems of organization, structure, methodology, and procedures remain unchanged.

Clandestine Collection was written by a life-long specialist in this profession, Samuel Halpern. Mr. Halpern served in the Office of Strategic Services (OSS) and the Strategic Services Unit (SSU) before joining CIA. There he served in a variety of posts before becoming Executive Assistant to the Deputy Director for Plans (the most senior official in the Clandestine Services) for seven years. In his essay Mr. Halpern, who retired in December 1974, maintained that the legal and organizational arrangements in the basic 1947 system as adjusted through the years, which leave collection, counterintelligence, and covert action together in CIA, are the most effective. Any other arrangement, he suggested, would be damaging to the mission. He argued further that collection capabilities had been seriously damaged by the Freedom of Information Act, the Congress, and the attitudes and guidelines adopted by recent Directors of Central Intelligence. As a consequence, the US lacked the capability to meet the needs of the immediate future, let alone the problems likely to face us in the late 1980's. Mr. Halpern went on to urge that a variety of corrective steps be taken at once to meet those needs.

The ensuing discussion dwelt at length, as it did in many of the sessions, on the legal and other restrictions inhibiting intelligence performance. Ways and means of ameliorating the situation were argued, although by and large there was endorsement of the idea of a somewhat freer hand for the intelligence agencies in carrying out their assigned tasks. It was recognized that the current public and institutional attitudes in the US regarding intelligence were negative and reflected a disinclination toward involvement in foreign matters. This was also seen as a reflection of the diminution of public confidence in governmental institutions, especially those involved in secrecy. No one foresaw immediate improvement in the situation.

Extensive discussion centered on the concept of reorganization. Yet it was generally agreed that no substantive changes should be made in the existing structure of the clandestine collection agencies without assurances that the end result would be better intelligence for the US. The need for the three clandestine disciplines—collection, counterintelligence, and covert action—to be retained in a single organization was stressed repeatedly by former professionals, on the grounds of their intimate interrelationship and the necessity for close control and direction under a central authority. Some participants disagreed and suggested that the other bureaucratic forms might produce superior results.

The somewhat improved environment in the US as it has affected American intelligence during the past two years is reflected in Mr. Halpern's essay as revised. He reiterates, however, his deeply felt concern that the system be strengthened to meet the bourgeoning requirements of this decade.

Counterintelligence at the Crossroads was written by Newton S. Miler, a former senior counterintelligence specialist who retired from CIA in December 1974. Mr. Miler argued that counterintelligence in the US is generally misunderstood, organizationally fragmented, hemmed in by legal and other restrictions, and—in sum—inadequate to deal with the threats of hostile espionage, covert action, terrorism, and sabotage that face the nation. An important measure contributing to this state of things was, as Mr. Miler described it, the elimination of CIA's centralized counterintelligence program which, from 1954 to 1973—and although no substitute for a national program—was the single component of the intelligence community serving the latter for purposes of CI overview and operational coordination. He held that unless those arrangements were reestablished and counterintelligence given the prominence it deserves, US intelligence as a whole would remain unable to meet the challenge of the 1980's. Finally, Mr. Miler suggested measures to be taken in the direction of a national counterintelligence program.

After agreeing that the counterintelligence function was vitally important, and that it could not be separated from the covert action and clandestine collection functions, the participants focused first on the extent of foreign espionage activity in the United States, and then on the restrictions imposed on counterintelligence in recent years through legislation or departmental guidelines. The Foreign

Intelligence Surveillance Act of 1978 was cited as being particularly onerous, and its pros and cons were discussed in detail.

Problems of coordination between the FBI and CIA were reviewed in terms of the differing responsibilities of the two organizations. Not all present agreed with Mr. Miler on the efficacy of the pre-1974 pattern of counterintelligence arrangements within CIA. Some took exception to his assessment of the management decisions that modified those arrangements, on grounds that they were appropriately designed to end the isolation of counterintelligence and bring it closer to the mainstream of clandestine service activity. Most former professionals felt that reorganization and new legislation were not likely to solve the overall counterintelligence problem.

In the revised version of his paper, Mr. Miler contends in even stronger terms that US counterintelligence is in disarray. The Reagan Administration's Executive Order 12333 in his opinion is completely inadequate. He is particularly disturbed at the continued exclusion of personnel, physical, document, and communications security programs—penetration of which are the primary objectives of any hostile intelligence action—from the purview of counterintelligence as defined. He is also deeply concerned at the government's apparent inability to understand counterintelligence, and at its unwillingness to come to grips with the nature and magnitude of the threat facing the US today.

Proceeding from these premises, Mr. Miler goes on to discuss in detail some of the unique features of counterintelligence, with emphasis on its objectives, disciplines, and functions. He proposes the establishment of a national counterintelligence program. On the other hand, he is opposed to creation of an independent counterintelligence agency, which he believes would segregate counterintelligence even more from the rest of the community. Instead, Mr. Miler urges a central coordinating responsibility for CIA, with the explicit endorsement of higher authority at the National Security Council and PFIAB (President's Foreign Intelligence Advisory Board) level for the evaluation of performance.

Failing the institution of substantive changes along the lines he has prescribed, Mr. Miler is frankly pessimistic about the US ability to meet the counterintelligence threat facing the country in the 1980's.

Covert Action was written by Hugh Tovar, who retired in 1978 having held several senior posts in CIA. In the earlier version of his paper, Mr. Tovar argued that US covert action capabilities had been eroded seriously during the upheaval of the 1970's. He discussed the concept of covert action in the American scheme of things, stressed its validity as an instrument of foreign policy, and suggested a possible framework for action to regain the old initiative and project it through the 1980's. Logical objectives were noted, as were certain of the techniques that might be employed against them—all of this depicted against the problems, legal and otherwise, that stood in the way of reversing the trend of the 1970's.

Participants in the discussion of covert action took note of the problem of determining when such activity should be undertaken. A definition of "importance" or "essentiality" was deemed useful, but probably impossible to achieve, given the position of some government officials who object to covert action in principle or on grounds that it is "counterproductive." Much attention was devoted to legislative restrictions, particularly the Hughes-Ryan Amendment, and the problem of confidence in the intelligence community at large resulting from repeated exposures.

There was some debate over whether paramilitary activity was an appropriate responsibility for CIA. Some participants questioned its utility and the Agency's ability to conduct it covertly; others argued that it is necessary and there is no other way to undertake it effectively.

For the most part, participants were positive on the need to recreate an effective covert action capability, in close conjunction with clandestine collection and counterintelligence as integral elements of US intelligence in the 1980's. The interdependence of the three disciplines was stressed repeatedly.

The current version of Mr. Tovar's essay has been expanded to include a more detailed account of the US covert action experience since World War II. It also suggests reasons for the success of some operations and the failure of others. Finally, addressing recent legislative developments and the issuance of a new executive order for the intelligence agencies, Mr. Tovar sees a distinct improvement in the atmospherics now bearing on covert action.

In the first edition of *Elements of Intelligence*, Dr. Michael M. Uhlmann discussed three broad approaches to the legal organization—and prospective reorganization—of US intelligence. At that time public debate focused on those questions. Restrictions and reform were the keynotes of discussion—whether in the context of executive orders, departmental guidelines, or charter legislation. By the end of 1979, the tenor of public exchanges on these subjects had altered radically. Most interested parties had come to agree, at least rhetorically, that the purpose of reform in the field of intelligence must be to improve the agencies' performance. Restrictions for the sake of restrictions appeared unwarranted.

Thus, one great obstacle to consideration of the theory and practice of US intelligence was removed. But another remained and with the passage of time loomed large—the tendency inherent in all professions to resist criticism of past performance, the urge to stand pat behind comfortable bureaucratic arrangements on the hopeful premise that change would create problems and would not produce improved results. Outsiders who are well disposed toward intelligence and wish to see a strong and effective US system may contend that the world is changing, and that along with it objectives, structures, and procedures hitherto deemed sacrosanct within the intelligence community may also have to change. The debate concerning intelligence in the 1980's will divide that group from some career people—possibly supported by outright opponents of major aspects of intelligence, such as the leaders of the American Civil Liberties Union—who also oppose change for varied and sometimes conflicting reasons.

Dr. Angelo Codevilla, a professional staff member of the Senate Intelligence Community since 1977, who also served on President Reagan's Transition Team for CIA, addresses these considerations in his paper, *Reforms and Proposal for Reform*. His review of developments since late 1979 covers the various attempts to legislate structural changes in the intelligence community and changes in certain of its basic procedures. Touching upon each of the intelligence disciplines and some of their special problems, Dr. Codevilla concludes that the government—the Executive Branch and Congress—have not yet faced up to the task of rigorously assessing the nation's present intelligence capability and of taking the steps necessary to ensure its adequacy to the requirements of the 1980's. Although Dr. Codevilla's essay postdates the other four, it provides a useful point of departure from which to review and study the many current questions posed by the other authors.

The views expressed in all five papers are, of course, those of the individual writers. They were presented, and are reproduced here, to help add another dimension to the public debate on intelligence. The papers should in no way be taken as representing the positions of any agency, department, or committee, although several of the authors, in accordance with their legal responsibilities, submitted the manuscripts for review before publication. It is encouraging to note that discussion of intelligence, which has moved through the stages of almost unquestioning acceptance in the 1950's and early 1960's, then the hostility and criticism in the 1970's, has in the main given way to a more balanced analysis of past activities and creative consideration of the needs of the 1980's. What follows is intended to contribute to that evolution.

CHAPTER ONE
Quality in US Intelligence

Daniel O. Graham

When the national debate over clandestine intelligence captured the headlines of the mid-1970's, the spotlight was on abuses, alleged or real, and on violations of American civil liberties by the intelligence agencies. Misuse of executive authority, interference in the national affairs of sovereign states, responsibility for bad policy decisions, these were far more titillating topics than the structure of the agencies or their professional performance as instrumentalities of the nation's foreign policy. The debate itself was focused on aspects of the clandestine arts. Analysis and estimates were ignored, as was the relationship between intelligence and policy. Far from evoking a serious look at current capabilities and future needs, public clamor focused on the values of an open society, and sharp questions were raised about the place of intelligence in the American ethical fabric.

This was understandable, given the temper of the times, but it obscured the very real need for an objective look at the several components of US intelligence—clandestine collection, counterintelligence, covert action and the analytic process, products, and organization. Critical questions about US intelligence were never asked. Just how well had it functioned during those years of political upheaval? Did it suffer as a result? Is it equipped to do the job required in the years ahead? There are no ready answers to these, but it is important that they be addressed. If one intelligence discipline malfunctions, the others are soon affected, often drastically, and the consequences for the nation can be dire. This is particularly true of intelligence estimates in their relation to policy information.

Crisis in Analysis

Some argued during those days of intense national debate that none of the intelligence disciplines was functioning well. Others pointed to analysis as the weakest element, and cited the failure of American intelligence to identify and evaluate the Soviet strategic build-up between 1975 and 1978 as portending far more serious consequences for the United States than the widely publicized abuses.

21

Thus questions about the scope and methods of analysis resurfaced. New attention was given to the kinds of organization, the attitudes, and the methods of recruiting, training, and motivating personnel that might lead to a better analytic capability.

All of this is in the right direction, but the process has barely begun. A bit of recent history will illustrate the dimensions of the problems as one practitioner has experienced it over the years.

Between 1975 and 1978, the intelligence community, in the face of massive information available to it concerning the size, scope, and purpose of the Soviet Union's strategic weapons building programs, repeatedly underestimated the significance of what was taking place. This became apparent in a succession of National Intelligence Estimates, which are the community's most important product, produced periodically or *ad hoc* as a collective effort over the signature of the Director of Central Intelligence. The track record of the NIEs on Soviet strategic arms was thus summarized in a dissenting opinion appended to the Senate Intelligence Committee's report on the so-called A-B Team affair in February 1978:

> While the Soviets were beginning the biggest military buildup in history, the NIEs judged that they would not try to build as many missiles as we had. When the Soviets approached our number, the NIEs said they were unlikely to exceed it substantially. When they exceeded it substantially, the NIEs said they would not try for decision superiority—the capability to fight and win a nuclear war. Only very recently have the NIEs admitted that possibility as an 'elusive question.' Now the NIEs say the Soviets may be trying for such a capability, but they cannot be sure if it will work.

In January of 1979, the nation learned from the *New York Times* that the current National Intelligence Estimate had recognized that the Soviet Union was indeed trying for the capability to win a nuclear war with minimal damage to itself, and that it was well on the way to achieving that capability. Unfortunately, the NIE came to this conclusion well after it had been reached by readers of most of this country's military and strategic publications and even *Commentary* magazine—roughly at about the time the *New Republic* did so. The nation has the right to expect more than that from its intelligence analysts working in concert on an issue of vital importance. Intelligence exists precisely to avoid rude awakenings such as this.

One could extend the list of intelligence failures to include Iran. As the Shah was rapidly losing his grip, a score of senior analysts at CIA were writing that Iran was not in a revolutionary situation, nor even in one that could be termed pre-revolutionary. In fact, they predicted that the Shah would rule well into the 1980's. It is hard to excuse such blindness, and we can only regret the effect on our policies during the years prior to the revolution. With the admitted advantage of hindsight, it would seem to have been within our capability to alert ourselves and our friends to likely trends. And if we could not buttress the latter fully against the inevitable, we might at least have refrained from proferring to them in December, 1978 and January, 1979 the advice that was to prove lethal to them.

Other failures can be argued with less dramatic overtones. This is not to say that the record of our analysts is one of unrelieved failure, nor that the level of analysis has always been below that of the information available to support it. There are success stories, some of them quite recent. The advance warning given in 1978-1979 of the Chinese invasion of Vietnam is one. Reporting on the Soviet invasion of Afghanistan is another, as was coverage of the refugee exodus from Cuba. But these do not alleviate the problem significantly. And the tragedy of intelligence failures such as the ones described is that they are quite avoidable. Typically, as in the case of the NIEs on Soviet strategic weapons, solid information is available, which could lead reasonable people to the correct conclusion. Moreover, such reasonable people have never been absent from the ranks of intelligence analysts. Throughout the decade during which the NIEs were so wrong about Soviet forces, there were some intelligence analysts, particularly in the Defense Intelligence Agency, who were right on the mark. There were even some analysts who dissented from the chorus of pollyannas in the intelligence community and said that the Shah of Iran was in deep trouble. However, the views of these analysts were unfortunately smothered and lost in exhaustive procedures in which the volumes of data the US received on the world, and the judgments which these data inspired in the minds of individual analysts were translated into finished intelligence.

During the compilation of an NIE, one agency may incorporate perceptive insights or relevant data in its own presentation. But in the endless interagency sessions which comprise the later stage of the estimate process those insights and data may be shunted aside, sent back for reconfirmation, or watered down because they do not fit another agency's position, or because they block inter-agency consensus on a particular point. The NIE in its final form is considered to represent the intelligence community. But it is forwarded over the signature of the Director of Central Intelligence and clearly must be acceptable to him. In short, the laborious process by which many views are formed into the intelligence view of the United States has not served the country well because it has resulted in a less accurate product.

Organizational Weaknesses

The problem with the analysis of intelligence is at least in part an organizational one, and organizational changes could well improve matters.

The original idea of the Board of National Estimates (BNE) was that national intelligence estimates were to be undertaken by an independent body not attached to intelligence agencies. However, the increases in the volume of technical data caused a corresponding growth in the need for expertise in this type of analysis. Experts were drawn from the staff analysts of the CIA's Office of National Estimates (ONE), and they came to regard appointment to the BNE as a very desirable promotion. Thus, when the CIA's ONE adopted the view that the Soviet threat was less important than they had previously thought, over a period of time this view also spread through the BNE.

The Central Intelligence Agency has some special bureaucratic imperatives of its own. On the one hand, it is intended to service the entire National Security Council and the Secretaries of State and Defense, as well as the Chairman of the Joint Chiefs of Staff. Yet the Secretary of Defense and the Chairman of the Joint Chiefs are also served by the Defense Intelligence Agency (DIA), while the Bureau of Intelligence and Research (INR) serves the Secretary of State. Thus there is constant friction between and among these three intelligence agencies. No solution to the problem has been proposed by the Congress or recent administrations. Indeed, the problem may be exacerbated if the power of the Director of Central Intelligence (DCI), who is also head of the CIA, is increased. This would effectively give the CIA domain over the Secretaries of State and Defense on intelligence matters, and further downgrade the input from other Departments.

A common sense solution would be to institutionalize competitive analysis. Since both technical data and the softer data from overt and clandestine sources are subject to different interpretations, competitive analysis would highlight the various possibilities. On a case-by-case basis, it also might be possible to reduce areas of disagreement, although data are sometimes inconclusive. (This is treated in greater detail below.)

Politics and the Conventional Wisdom

None of this is meant to discount the continuing importance of managerial, personal, and intellectual factors that bear on the process. It can be argued that the analysts are often preoccupied with staying close and visible to the policymakers. They are busy with special estimates, memoranda, briefing pieces suggested by themselves or requested by the policymakers. These can, and sometimes do, bog down the analyst and detract from time he could better apply to steeping himself in the substance of his tasks. Intelligence analysis, and this may also affect the collection process in the form of short-term *ad hoc* demands for information is thus reduced to the level of not-very-good journalism.

But an even greater barrier to sound analysis lies in the mind of the analyst. It is the power of "conventional wisdom." Let us say we know that the Soviets conduct three-quarters of their tests on ICBMs during business hours Monday through Friday, and if we observe two-thirds of these, we will have observed half of Soviet tests, and can safely extrapolate our knowledge to the other half. Another example may be summed up by statements such as these: Telemetry of missile tests is the standard way for the Soviets to learn about their own tests. Therefore they will not learn about them any other way. Therefore if we read x percent of the Soviets' telemetry, we know x percent about Soviet tests.

This is nonsense. For intelligence based on such rigid perceptions to be effective, the target would have to be more stupid than the Soviets have proved to be. Yet another example, perhaps the most dangerous one, is the belief that if information on a particular item satisfies the official intelligence requirements for that item, then we know all we need to know about it. Admittedly, analysis of intelligence and bureaucratic routine are mortal enemies.

Political considerations are also the mortal enemies of good intelligence analysis. The very possibility that a high-level policymaker might send a paper back to an agency indicating he did not like the conclusion all too often sends chiefs and sub-chiefs scurrying, trying to shade their judgments. The very perception of political interest can create controversy based upon very little substantive difference. The controversy over the role and range of the Soviets' backfire bomber is as good an example as one could want of a difference of opinion which exists because there are high-level customers for the different views. No one disagreed on the airplane's physical characteristics. No one contended that an airplane with such a range could fly from Soviet territory to American territory without refueling. The refueling probes were visible to all analysts. Yet there was disagreement over whether the airplane had intercontinental range. This is not an argument for eliminating differences of opinion which are based on political considerations, quite the contrary. We should recognize that they are inevitable, and that they can even be healthy in the right organizational context.

The Stimulus of Change

There is much to be said for organizational change as a means of alleviating the troubles that affect the analytic process. The stimulus of change is often conducive to a better product. And yet almost any organizational pattern can be effective as long as the analysts themselves are well qualified, trained, and free of the fetters of conventional wisdom. It helps also if their managers are wise, and if their political superiors do their duty in keeping politics out of analysis. This is obviously a large order, and one that acts of Congress can do little to bring into existence.

Consider two events in 1976. Pursuant to a suggestion by the President's Foreign Intelligence Advisory Board, a team of independent analysts was given access to the intelligence community's data on Soviet strategic arms. This so-called B-Team concluded that the NIEs had been grossly underestimating Soviet developments and intentions. After some agonizing, the authors of the NIEs, unable to produce evidence to contradict the B-Team, changed their own position. Also in 1976, an independent analyst showed that the CIA changed its estimates. Whether the original CIA positions on these issues reflected bad management, ossified thinking, a response to political considerations, or simply bad analysis is immaterial. The important thing is that the pressure of competition widened the arena and gave the decisionmakers of both executive and legislative branches the opportunity to make responsible choices in the face of differing viewponts.

Not all policymakers welcome opportunities of this type. Some find the responsibility for making a judgment unpleasantly onerous, and prefer a single estimate, one which in effect resolves their doubts eloquently, if simplistically.

The Case for Competitive Analysis

Competitive analysis is opposed by many in the intelligence community. Some object on grounds of managerial efficiency; others because it might lead to the dismemberment of the CIA as we know it—that is to say, as an intelligence mechanism that does a little bit of everything. Their point is well taken. Since 1947 intelligence has changed, and CIA has developed in ways which argue for disentangling the CIA's various functions and reaffirming its original and unique functions. No one should shrink from doing something which would be to the country's advantage mainly to spare the sensibilities of an organization. Intelligence and CIA are not synonymous.

The CIA's original core, its primary responsibility, was clandestine collection of foreign intelligence and covert action in support of US foreign policy. The broader the scope of CIA activity became, the more difficult it became to preserve the secrecy required for its critical missions. Agency involvement in the development and management of large technical systems (e.g., the Glomar Explorer), with all the requisite contact with industry, contractors, labor, operating crews, and the like further weakens its ability to protect that which *must* be clandestine.

CIA has long visualized itself as the paramount influence in American intelligence. Agency analysts have often been unfairly critical of the military services on the premise that the latter produce self-serving intelligence, and that their inflated conclusions can be reduced to perspective only through the cool medium of CIA's analytic process. Over the years, CIA has successfully defended its position, and notwithstanding a remarkable record of underestimation of the Soviet armed forces, has gained some legislative support for an even greater centralization of the intelligence community, looking toward the establishment of a Director of National Intelligence, who would also be Director of the CIA. Inevitably, this would lead to still further absorption by CIA of the intelligence activities of other agencies, and would fly in the face of many years' experience.

If the intelligence community is indeed to be reorganized through legislation or otherwise, it is imperative that the functions of the head of CIA and the overseer of the total US intelligence effort be separated; CIA's function must be more narrowly focused on the critical and highly sensitive field of clandestine intelligence abroad and covert action.

Against these proposals, it is generally argued that intelligence community coordination responsibility could not be carried out, whether by a Director of Central Intelligence, or by a Director of National Intelligence if the latter were separated from the CIA as his "institutional base." such is often the contention of CIA spokesmen resisting the idea of any diminution of the Agency's present dominance. The argument is vulnerable, given recent experience. No one would say that Henry Kissinger, prior to his appointment as Secretary of State, lacked power because he had only a small National Security Council staff and no "institutional base." Direct access to the President, to the Congress, and to the NSC ought to provide a Director with all the authority he requires, obviating the need for a personal bureaucratic power base.

The Case Against Monopoly

Most important, neither the CIA, nor the Pentagon, nor any Director of National Intelligence, nor any single bureaucracy should monopolize analysis of the mountains of information the United States receives. It is less important to decide where the analytical resources of the intelligence community should be located than to decide that there should be more than one location, with equal resources and equal access to the nation's policymakers. There are various ways in which this could be accomplished. The Defense Intelligence Agency might be strengthened and given greater independence. The analytic side of CIA could be removed from the Directorate of Operations and possibly divided into two agencies. These in turn might be strengthened with assets that belong to DIA. The efficacy of most such approaches is certain to be questioned; opinions differ widely, and are strongly held. The important thing is that the issue be scrutinized and steps taken to avoid perpetuation of specific features of the existing intelligence system, which in the opinion of this observer, have not served us well.

CHAPTER TWO

Clandestine Collection

Samuel Halpern

This essay is designed to introduce the reader to one of the major elements of intelligence, clandestine collection. It does not treat in detail all types of intelligence collection. Information, for example, derived from publicly available sources is not discussed, although it comprises the great bulk of intelligence collected and used by the government.

The main concern here is with information that is protected because of its importance or sensitivity, and therefore accessible only through clandestine means. The paper is focused on the status of clandestine collection as a function, and on its future tasks and needs as we continue into the 1980's.

Espionage

The term "clandestine collection," first of all, is another way of saying "espionage," entailing the use of both human sources and technical devices such as "bugs" emplaced by humans. In other words it is old fashioned spying, the recruitment of agents and manipulation of people. Clandestine collection is costly in terms of time and manpower, unlike covert action which usually requires a larger expenditure of money as well. Clandestine collection requires a long lead time to identify and recruit those human sources who might have access to the required information. There are no quick fixes. It is a slow and laborious process which is used only as a last resort.

There are ways of supplementing the standard techniques of espionage, for example, through cooperation with the intelligence services of friendly countries, which can be very useful sources of information. So, too, it is often fruitful to draw upon information in the possession of refugees, emigres, and defectors. Less obvious but nonetheless of potential importance in a collection program, businessmen with foreign interests and associations can be drawn upon discretely to share their knowledge and insights with the government.

The term "clandestine collection" applies also to information collected by the great variety of technical means now available. Information thus collected is intrinsically secret or hidden. Sources from which the data are collected are generally protected. Ideally, those sources should remain unaware that the information has been collected. Practical and bureaucratic organizational considerations, such as the greater expense of technical collection systems and the fact that they are more varied and complex than human sources, has necessitated separate handling and processing of the information produced. Thus the term "clandestine collection" is used to denote not only espionage but also information collected from a vast range of scientific and technical systems. Any serious discussion of the subject must encompass both.

Technical Collection

This field has mushroomed over the years. It is no longer restricted to photography—whether by the hand-held camera in slow-moving aircraft of World War I, the later U-2 or SR 71 "spy" planes, or even today's overhead reconnaissance. Nor is it confined to communications intelligence, exemplified by the success in World War II of the British and American reading respectively of German and Japanese encrypted military and diplomatic radio messages. The 1978 Annual Report of the House Permanent Select Committee on Intelligence listed more than a dozen different technical intelligence systems.

Signals intelligence (SIGINT), for example, includes the sub-disciplines of communications intelligence (COMINT) and electronic intelligence (ELINT). Comint is concerned with interception of radio signals, both enciphered and cleartext. Elint is the collection of machine-generated signals, as in the case of rockets and fire control systems they employ. Photographic intelligence (PHOTINT) devolves on more than one sub-discipline, including the interpretation of photographic, infrared, and radar imaging systems, wherein film and electro-optical means are used to recover the various forms of energy reflected by objects in order to form visual images. Acoustics intelligence is yet another of the complex collection techniques that have assumed increasing importance in recent years.

Human vs. Technical Sources

These and other technical systems produce vast quantities of data of all types that no human collectors can match. This has led some commentators to suggest that we can rely solely on technical collection and avoid the use of clandestine collection with its exploitation of human beings and the possible danger of exposure and compromise. Indeed, as former Deputy Director of Central Intelligence, Admiral Bobby R. Inman, said in an interview with the *New York Times* on July 5, 1982, "There was a period of time when decisionmakers believed that satellite photography was going to answer all our needs."

Admiral Inman, however, went on to say, "We're all a little wiser now. No analyst should be left dependent on a single means of acquiring intelligence. Human collection runs the risk of relying on someone who wants to mislead you. Technical collection may leave you without access to certain things or without a context for understanding some report." It is thus quite clear that all systems of collection, ranging from newspapers, radio and television, academic reports and studies, business and embassy reporting on the one hand, and extending to technical and human source reporting on the clandestine side are important and potentially useful. No single system of collection is adequate. All complement one another.

Technical collection has provided at least one direct benefit to the human collector: he has been freed to concentrate on the high priority targets which can provide key intelligence on intentions, and on the political and economic developments which we need to know about. Thus the human collector is in a position to expend minimal effort collecting routine geographic and other such data. But clandestine collection is still a limited tool, to be used as a rifle and not as a shotgun. And by the same token, technical collection and the vast resources it has made available have given rise to a concomitant problem which the analysts are still hard pressed to cope with, namely, the sheer quantity of data flowing into the system. It is obviously imperative that the collectors of both categories of information and the analysts who work with their product realize their interdependence and coordinate their efforts toward the common end.

If, and it is a big if, the other agencies and departments of government do their job of reporting on foreign areas, then clandestine collection need not provide more than five to ten percent of the data available to the analysts on areas which are open societies, and about double that on closed societies. With the increasing number of countries becoming closed societies, particularly in the Third World, there will be even greater need in the 1980's for clandestine collection of information. It has a limited but important use, for while it is not the major source in quantity of information sought by the analysts and policymakers, it often provides the key or significant piece of information needed for full understanding of the subject. In the early 1970's, the Directorate for Intelligence (DDI) of CIA found that about 30% of key and significant information used in its finished intelligence studies and reports came from clandestine sources.[1] That indicates that the other agencies and departments of government were not doing their collection jobs, with resulting misuse of the clandestine collectors who should be concentrating on the important information not otherwise obtainable.

Collection Targets in the 1980's

Inasmuch as the Soviet Union is still the only power that can inflict physical damage on the US, it remains the prime target for clandestine collection. But it cannot be the only target. Other areas such as the Middle East, China, and Western Europe are of vital concern to the US. Clandestine collection methods must be applied in those and any other areas where there are intelligence gaps.

In the 1980's the US will continue to need information on Soviet plans and intentions in the political and military sector, its internal and external activities, and especially on its use of surrogate forces in areas such as Africa, the Middle East, and Latin America. Other key requirements will include:

- The Middle East and other oil-producing areas and their plans and intentions to exploit oil for political purposes.

- China's progress in modernization; relations with the Soviet Union; internal political situation.

- The continued cohesion of NATO as a defensive alliance against the Soviets.

- Scientific and technological advancements, including the problems of nuclear proliferation and technology transfer from the West to the Soviet Union and its friends and allies.

---

[1]Senate Select Committee on Intelligence. National Reorganization and Reform Act of 1978. Hearings before the Select Committee on Intelligence of the US Senate, 95th Congress, 2nd Session on S.2525, April 4, 5, 19, 25; May 3, 4, 16; June 15, 21; July 11, 18, 20; and August 3, 1978. US Government Printing Office, Washington, 1978, p. 117. Statement on April 25, 1978 by Mr. Thomas H. Karamessines, the Assistant Deputy Director for Plans, Central Intelligence Agency, 1962-1967, and Deputy Director for Plans, Central Intelligence Agency, 1967-1973.

- The political and economic stability of our allies and powers closely associated with us, and of the neutral or Third World countries.
- Terrorism, both international and local, particularly as it affects our friends and allies.

Basically, US intelligence requirements concerning events abroad will continue along existing lines. The responsibility of policymakers will be to refine and specify their needs. To meet the latter through the techniques of clandestine collection, our intelligence services would profit by a period of stability and quiet. A moratorium on organizational and personnel changes would be most helpful. Taking note of the various proposals for revamping the CIA in particular and the intelligence community as a whole, the clandestine collection function should be retained as part of CIA. It should not be separated from the other intelligence disciplines of counterintelligence and covert action. All these are interlocked and mutually supporting. Covert action depends on good intelligence and cannot be conducted in a vacuum, while counterintelligence is essential to conduct either clandestine collection or covert action. Any juggling of the location in the intelligence community of these three interdependent disciplines would only make them a new target of the media, and would be extremely unsettling. To avoid unnecessary duplication, the Director of Central Intelligence should continue to coordinate the foreign clandestine collection activities of the military service and the FBI with those of CIA.

Strengthening US Intelligence

One way to rebuild confidence among foreigners, official and non-official, who are disposed to cooperate with the US is to ensure the ability to protect sources and methods. Without some visible signs that sources can be protected, it will be difficult at best, if not impossible, to convince foreigners, both officials and ordinary citizens, that they can work for the US without being exposed. The Deputy Director of Central Intelligence (DDCI), Mr. Frank Carlucci, testified before the House Intelligence Committee's legislative sub-committee on April 5, 1979, that the CIA was losing valuable information because foreign and domestic sources feared exposure under the FOIA. Other high level intelligence officials, including former

DDCI Inman and DCI William J. Casey have made similar statements about the effect of the current FOIA.

American business, which can provide both cover and information, and foreign intelligence services are simply unable and unwilling to cooperate as fully as they once did because of the present provisions of the FOIA, including the fact that under legal review procedures US courts can release classified data previously denied to a requester by CIA. While it is true that as of the last quarter of 1982 the courts have not released such data, the possibility of such release exists as long as the FOIA provisions are not changed. As then DDCI Carlucci said, the FOIA "has called into question around the world our ability to keep a secret." This alone makes it imperative to change the FOIA. The principles of need-to-know and compartmentation need re-emphasis. That means endorsing the secrecy agreement on current and former employees not only in CIA but throughout the intelligence community, and reducing the amount and types of information released under the Freedom of Information Act (FOIA).

There are no substitutes for hiring good people to become intelligence officers who can work with foreigners abroad. This will require continued and renewed relationships with colleges and universities to spot likely candidates for employment. Some of these relationships must be secret so as not to destroy the cover of prospective employees. The same would apply to American business and other institutions where possible recruits might be expected. If Americans who are willing to cooperate with their government wish that relationship to be protected, their wishes should be respected.

To become an experienced intelligence officer takes several years. This would include training, at least one tour of duty of two to three years at headquarters and a similar period abroad, roughly five to seven years. Some obviously desirable attributes for candidates are area knowledge and language proficiency. They should also have initiative, be career-minded, and willing to accept anonymity. These latter qualities are particularly essential and often overlooked. The people now being hired will be the intelligence officers in the late 1980's. Until then we must rely on the officers employed previously. There is some question now, following upon the heavy attrition through retirement and resignation during the 1970's, as to whether there are enough experienced officers left on duty to meet current requirements. If so, then the requirements must be trimmed lest people be spread too thin. Users of intelligence information are prone to overlook the number of officers needed both here and abroad to cover each foreign area adequately. Too often requirements are added to existing requirements without regard for the totality of the impact on the clandestine collector. It is human nature to do the easy things first before the difficult things. This plus the pressure for quick intelligence results has often led in practice to operations officers relegating the hard targets to a lower priority. They must be pursued continuously, even if it means no immediately visible collection results.

Cover for Intelligence Collection

The intense publicity of the mid-1970's had a very damaging impact on official cover—that delicate figleaf of protection intelligence personnel must have in order to function effectively abroad. Official cover in particular needs diversification; it should be extended to all departments and agencies of the government which have overseas representation. Much more use should be made of non-official cover, including proprietary mechanisms created specifically for the task at hand. This is, of course, rendered very difficult when broad categories of persons such as journalists and academicians are proscribed from helping their country clandestinely. On its own, the CIA in the past has always excluded humanitarian organizations such as the Red Cross, CARE, UNICEF, Rockefeller Foundation, Ford Foundation and, despite reports to the contrary, the Peace Corps and Fulbright Scholars from use in any clandestine or covert activities, including cover. If the trend towards exemption by categories continues, there will soon be no viable non-official cover available. The job of the clandestine collector would thus become impossible.

Congressional Oversight

Externally, while the question of Charter legislation for the intelligence community has been laid to rest for the present, interest in the subject is far from dead. Were it to revive, it would lead to more disquiet and another period of uncertainty. Congress has shown that it can handle any problems by amending existing legislation on a case-by-case basis. This approach is preferable to attempting to draft a comprehensive charter, listing what the intelligence community should and should not do. Obviously, the fewer restrictions on clandestine collection the better, lest we end up with a service so hobbled as to be completely ineffective. This is not the place to discuss the subject of restrictions in detail. It is the place, however, to highlight the fact that if the intelligence service were thus in effect hamstrung, it might be better not to have an intelligence service at all. Policy-makers would then be spared the embarrassment of relying on an illusory capability, a service that for all practical purposes has been reduced to the level of a facade. A costly side effect of this would be to spare us the charge of "intelligence failure" whenever an unpre-dicted (or unpredictable) event occurs in the world. But at least it would be known and understood that the US walked with blinders in foreign affairs.

Over the several years that the Senate and House Intelligence Committees have been in existence, their record for keeping secrets has been at least as good as that of the Executive branch. Both committees, however, will have to make every effort to keep partisan politics out of the subject of intelligence. Nothing could be more damaging than to make intelligence a partisan political football.

While the present system of two committees has apparently worked well, a preferable alternative would be a single joint committee with a joint staff. This would go a long way in showing foreigners who might be willing to work with the US that Congress is interested in limiting knowledge about intelligence activities to the bare minimum. It would also help if other committees of Congress such as Govern-ment Operations and Judiciary, but not Appropriations, were to give up their right to inquire into those aspects of intelligence activities which fall within their legislative jurisdiction. Congress could be served quite adequately by the one joint committee or, as at present, the existing Intelligence Committees, for oversight of intelligence activities. Knowledge of the latter should be restricted to those committees only, and sensitive operational data should not be made available to all members of Congress. The security procedures in Congress seem to have inhibited members from taking advantage of their access to the classified information. Yet the opportunity for inadvertent or deliberate disclosure exists. Congressmen should be willing to allow the intelligence committees to act as their surrogates on these matters.

In mid-1982, Congress and President Reagan took a concrete step in expressing public support for intelligence activity by passing and signing into law the Intelligence Identities Protection Act. Other legislation needed to limit the diffusion of sensitive information, in addition to revision of FOIA, would include protection of intelligence sources and methods from unauthorized disclosure and revision of the espionage statutes. All would enhance the intelligence effort. The fact that the US engages in intelligence activities abroad has been officially acknowledged, so there is no need to pretend that the US does not engage in espionage. There might even come a day when the government would publicly honor an intelligence officer, just as the Soviets honored Richard Sorge and "Colonel Rudolph Abel." Such an event would be a morale booster for those engaged in intelligence.

Outlook for the 1980's

A prime requisite abroad is the rebuilding of our relationships with foreign intelligence and security services. Much of this will depend on some of the steps suggested above, especially on limiting the knowledge of such relations to the barest minimum. Foreign services, whose help in the past has been most valuable, need assurance that any working arrangements with them will not become widely known.

In general, the intelligence needs of the 1980's will involve a long rebuilding process. There are no instant foreign assets that can be found to provide the information needed by the policymakers. We will have to rely on those officers currently available to recruit new assets and mount new intelligence collection operations or extend existing ones. New officers will have to be employed and trained and given experience so that by the middle and late 1980's they will be able to expand our collection capabilities and provide for continuity in the 1980's and beyond. This decade will also be the time to build new cover and new relations abroad. On the human side, the cost of meeting current requirements while hiring and training new people should be about the same as in the mid-1970's, with the addition of the inflation factor. This applies to personnel salaries, cover mechanisms and the technical equipment such as surveillance aids, agent communications, and the like. By keeping the service small and proceeding at a measured pace, budgets for clandestine collection can be kept within reason.

Technical collection contrasts sharply with collection through human sources. It is inherently more costly, and subject to frequent change in proportion to state-of-the-art developments. We must assume the aggregate budgetary pressures will have a restrictive effect on technical collection, although at this distance it is impossible to assess it precisely.

The outlook for intelligence now is better than it was in the mid and late 1970's, but the future is by no means assured. Budget cuts and fiscal restraints alluded to above may affect all intelligence activities adversely, including clandestine collection. Changing attitudes in the Congress might again introduce a situation comparable to that of the late 1970's when the FBI was denied an increase of 125 positions to try to cope with the espionage and counterintelligence threat posed by the increasing number of Soviets in this country. Many new and inexperienced people are now engaged in intelligence activities; they need time to mature. The chilling effect on initiatives in intelligence that dates back to the exposures and criticisms of the mid 1970's is still being felt. The Attorney General guidelines, even though they may be modified somewhat, are an example. All of these including the general draw-down of intelligence capabilities of recent years, make the near future a time when more rather than fewer so-called "intelligence failures" are conceivable. As former DDCI Admiral Inman said to the *New York Times*, "Our major weaknesses include a minimal effort both in collection and analysis about many of the non-Communist countries. We lack the encyclopedic effort that will let us understand trends before we get to the level of a crisis."

No Easy Solutions

An example of a problem of collection (and of analysis) was the situation in Iran in the late 1970's, leading to the overthrow of the Shah. It was as much a policy failure as it was an intelligence failure, as the House Intelligence Committee reported. It is also unrealistic to expect the US to know more about a country than the secret police of that country. More officers with experience and language capability, plus a willingness on the part of the policymakers to take the risk of dealing with the "outs" as well as with the "ins," might limit the surprises but cannot eliminate them. The US cannot deploy as many people as a secret police can to collect information in a police state. Here too it should be recognized that leaders of police states are no different from analysts and leaders of open states when it comes to ignoring clandestinely acquired information in making policy. Hitler disregarded the information provided by his agent "Cicero," a butler to the British ambassador in Turkey in World War II. Stalin paid no attention to Richard Sorge's (and others') warnings that Germany would attack Russia in June 1941. President Kennedy was unimpressed by early reports of strategic missiles being emplaced in Cuba in 1962, and his successors, Johnson and Nixon made their own interpretations of information on events in Vietnam. The wide gap between collection of raw information and its interpretation by analysts and policymakers is often overlooked. Secret police in police states can and do collect voluminous quantities of raw data which no outside service can duplicate. But they do not relinquish it readily, and even agent penetrations of secret police services can only provide a relatively small amount of the information available to the service.

If US intelligence cannot duplicate, in terms of sheer quantity, the raw data in the files of, say, Savak, the internal security service of the Shah's government in Iran; or if full access to the intelligence and security files of the South African government is, understandably, not available to us, that is no excuse for failing to know if the political leadership of those countries is receiving the available information and is, or is not, ignoring it. This necessitates effective liaison with local intelligence and security services, agent penetration of those services, and penetration of non-governmental groups in any country of interest. Lastly, it only makes sense to demand that US intelligence know precisely what a third country service—particularly the KGB, if applicable, may be doing in a given country, be it Iran, Saudi Arabia, Ethiopia, Mexico, or whichever. These are not easy tasks.

And legislation, though important as noted above, is not the panacea many people think it to be. The best way it can help intelligence is to limit the restrictions which were imposed in the late 1970's, and to reduce the number of people who have access to information on sensitive sources and methods. Legislation is not needed to provide incentives for intelligence officers. Existing procedures already provide for honor and merit awards, and even financial awards, for outstanding work.

There is no certain or easy way to collect intelligence clandestinely. Dealing with human sources is a matter of continuing to try and try again. It also means knowing how, and being ready, to take advantage of opportunities such as defections. It means having the necessary clandestine mechanisms in place in order to move quickly. As we proceed further into the 1980's in an increasingly turbulent world, we must persevere in rebuilding an intelligence service able to collect information from clandestine and other sources in response to steadily burgeoning requirements.

CHAPTER THREE

Counterintelligence at the Crossroads

Newton S. Miler

The US is on the horns of a dilemma. Foreign intelligence agents operate in our midst, and we are faced with a hostile adversary. Defensive measures remain inadequate in the face of criticism by those who view them as endangering civil liberties. Counterintelligence is thus hamstrung, ill-defended and misunderstood, organizationally fragmented and unequal to the task of protecting our institutions.

If this condition is ever to be rectified, counterintelligence must be seen in full perspective—as a vital element of the nation's security system, the essential underpinning not only for an effective foreign policy but for protection of our free institutions as well. A centralized approach to counterintelligence is imperative. This need not entail subordination of all counterintelligence disciplines and functions under the mantle of a "super" agency. But there must be a central vantage point from which these can be viewed and coordinated. And this can be accomplished without encroaching upon American civil liberties.

The will and ability of the Soviet Union to project its power is now widely recognized. In time this should lead to a revitalization of US counterintelligence, but the task will not be easy. There is still confusion over "domestic intelligence," and misunderstanding of the complexities of true national counterintelligence. After weighing the lessons of the past for their bearing on the present, the US will have to decide on the kind of counterintelligence program it deems necessary to meet the challenge facing the nation today.

The Dilemma

The definition of counterintelligence currently in use in the US today is spelled out in Executive Order 12333 of December 4, 1981.

Counterintelligence means information gathered and activities conducted to *protect* against espionage and other intelligence activities, sabotage, or assassinations conducted for or on behalf of foreign powers, organizations or persons, or international terrorist activities, *but not including personnel*, physical, document, or communications security programs.

This wording follows verbatim that employed by the Carter Administration in its Executive Order 12036 of January 24, 1978. The two

45

orders contrast strikingly with the definition of counterintelligence that guided previous administrations, set forth originally in National Security Council Intelligence Directive No. 5 of April 21, 1958, repeated in NSCID No. 5 dated January 18, 1961, and again in NSCID No. 5 dated January 17, 1972.[1]

> Counterintelligence is defined as that intelligence activity, with its resultant product, devoted to *destroying the effectiveness* of inimical foreign intelligence activities and undertaken *to protect* the security of the nation and its personnel, information, and installations against espionage, sabotage, and subversion. Counterintelligence includes the process of procuring, developing, recording, and disseminating information concerning hostile clandestine activity and of penetrating, manipulating, or repressing individuals, groups, or organizations conducting such activity.

The differences between these directives—some of them obvious, others rather subtle—illustrate the intelligence dilemma in which the US government now finds itself. Under the Carter Administration and with subsequent endorsement by the Reagan Administration, counterintelligence was redefined and circumscribed. Where once it was recognized as a vital element of intelligence and directed to perform aggressively and comprehensively on a wide front against threats to national security, counterintelligence is today essentially passive, reactive, and narrowly limited in terms of authority to collect and retain basic information and in the employment of investigative and operational resources. The reasons for this revised definition and sharply restricted approach were political and philosophical. It was feared that counterintelligence unchecked posed a greater danger to the nation than foreign espionage.

It was ironic that the Carter executive order should have become effective hardly a year after Christopher John Boyce and Andrew Daulton Lee were arrested for espionage on behalf of the Soviet Union (January 16, 1977). Having successfully circumvented the routine security and counterespionage processes established to prevent foreign intelligence penetration into sensitive intelligence and

---

[1]A National Security Council Intelligence Directive was a classified, sensitive document dealing with an important policy matter and understood to carry the force of presidential approval. It conveyed instructions to the senior levels of government upon whose responsibilities the NSCID impinged. As a rule it was followed up with further issuances at lower government echelons, spelling out in detail the intended action. In contrast, an Executive Order is normally an unclassified document intended for public consumption. It can be argued whether a sensitive subject such as counterintelligence can be treated effectively in a document of this type.

defense installations, Boyce and Lee revealed communications security secrets to the Soviets, removed or photographed classified documents, and moved with ease through physical security checkpoints carrying incriminating documents and equipment. They were never subjected to continuing personnel security assessment. One may speculate also on whether the ineffectiveness of US counterintelligence efforts overseas might not have enabled Boyce and Lee to continue undetected as long as they did.

The extensive damage these spies perpetrated was well documented by January 24, 1978, and the security and counterespionage weaknesses which let this come about were manifest. Although the need for a strengthened counterintelligence program could not have been clearer, the new definition of counterintelligence removed from its cognizance the very security programs which demonstrably needed improvement.

Understanding Counterintelligence

That the government in 1978 could promulgate an unrealistic, self-defeating definition of counterintelligence is not surprising. The nation was still in a period when anti-intelligence—especially anti-counterintelligence—attitudes were very strong. Both the Executive branch and the Congress entertained a naïve conception of the Soviet threat. The media, supporting the vocal anti-intelligence elements in US society, promoted an atmosphere in which it was difficult for objective, much less pro-intelligence, viewpoints to get a fair hearing. Indeed, there were moments when, in the face of congressional attempts to circumscribe presidential authority, there seemed to be some serious question whether the US would have *any* future intelligence activity worthy of the name.

Suffice it to say that US intelligence was devastated during the mid to late 1970's, and is still in disarray. The reasons, the motives, and the impact of action and policy decisions on the part of both the Executive and the Congress remain arguable. The fact is that the US lost sight of its basic intelligence needs. Nor has it fully regained focus to date. US intelligence capabilities today are less than first-rate.

A dismaying reflection of this failure to regain focus can be seen in the Reagan Administration's adherence to its predecessors' definition of counterintelligence. It is thus evident that the US does not understand how counterintelligence responsibilities and functions must be programmed in order to maintain internal security and support the development of a first-rate intelligence system. It is equally clear that the hostile foreign intelligence threat has not been assessed realistically against the full spectrum of Soviet strategy. There is no doubt that the Reagan Administration recognizes that the Soviets are indeed an implacable foe, that they are fully prepared to insert their policy views into US foreign and domestic dialogues, and that the number of Soviet bloc spies in the US and their success in stealing our technological and defense secrets is a serious threat. Yet this concern has never been translated into a comprehensive and coherent national counterintelligence program.

The reasons why this has not been done range from an unwillingness to face the inevitable anti-intelligence opposition, revived and stimulated by the media, to a more basic problem of understanding true counterintelligence. There is another consideration, however, which may be even more fundamental: the government has been unable to decide whether the US should have a *centralized* counterintelligence program, or should go on trying to develop an effective program through a system of *decentralized* responsibilities and functions.

The origins of this peculiarly counterintelligence problem date back to 1973, some 18 months before the concerted media and congressional attacks on the intelligence community began. The CIA, in a unilateral and apparently routine internal reorganization, dismantled its own national counterintelligence program framework. Counterintelligence within the Agency was in effect decentralized.

This action, a root cause underlying many of the counterintelligence problems facing the nation, has been lost sight of in the confusion surrounding the Executive and Congressional investigations and actions pursuant to the *New York Times* publication in December 1974 of allegations concerning misdeeds and illegalities committed by CIA within the US or against US citizens. There is no doubt that Executive and Congressional action during the period 1975 to 1980 severely handicapped and complicated the implementation of counterintelligence activities. But if the US is ever to put its house in order and then proceed to contend with the other factors which restrict and inhibit counterintelligence, it must address the act which dismantled the centralized national framework of counterintelligence within CIA and which in turn had a profoundly adverse effect on

American intelligence and national security. The full impact of this event on the counterintelligence capability of the nation has yet to be understood, and indeed it may never be until a catastrophic espionage, subversive, or terrorist incident forces a reluctant government to address its dimensions.

It is difficult, of course, for the government, and for the intelligence community in particular, to admit that for nearly a decade the US has not had a counterintelligence program worthy of the name. Nevertheless, if the government is to fulfill its national security responsibilities, this fact must be acknowledged. Counterintelligence must be put into its proper perspective as a key element of national defense. The counterintelligence house must be put in order. The negative image of counterintelligence must be corrected and an explanation given as to why it is vital and what it is designed to do for the nation.

In Search of a New Definition

The first step toward putting counterintelligence into perspective is to define properly and describe this intelligence discipline. The present governmental definition is misleading, confusing, and inaccurate because it does not delineate the types of information and activity essential to any effective counterintelligence program. It merely delineates certain of the limits of information gathering and of investigative and operational activities which the government since early 1978 has deemed permissible counterintelligence functions. It not only distorts perception of the actual foreign intelligence threat, but also removes from counterintelligence purview the very programs which are primary targets for foreign espionage. The net effect of this exclusion is severely to restrict, if not totally eviscerate, US counterespionage.

The NSCID definition is apolitical; it explains the positive purpose of counterintelligence, and indicates the functional responsibilities necessary to achieve the purpose. It embraces, without specifying, every consideration needed to protect the nation from hostile clandestine activity, foreign or domestic, and it implicitly recognizes that counterintelligence is fundamental in protecting the nation's personnel, information (documents), installations (physical) and, by extension, the means by which information is exchanged (communications).

This is an excellent definition, but one not likely to be resurrected—in part because it carries a political stigma, but also because it characterizes counterintelligence as an aggressive intelligence responsibility, and one that cannot be fulfilled if government security programs are excluded from its purview. Furthermore, it implies that a centralized counterintelligence system is necessary to collate information and provide coordinated operational guidance designed to destroy hostile foreign intelligence activity. It could, and indeed did, serve as an operational guideline, and therefore may be too specific to serve as a basic definition.

A less aggressively worded and apolitical definition, which not only explains counterintelligence, provides a foundation for a national program, and would serve as a permanent yardstick to measure the effectiveness of future counterintelligence efforts, is the following:

> Counterintelligence (CI) is the national effort to prevent foreign intelligence services and foreign-controlled political movements (which are often supported by the intelligence services) from infiltrating our institutions and establishing the potential to engage in espionage, subversion, terrorism, and sabotage. Counterintelligence involves investigations and surveillance activities to detect and neutralize the foreign intelligence service presence, the collation of information about foreign intelligence services and the initiation of operations to penetrate, disrupt, deceive, and manipulate these services and related organizations to our advantage.

This definition sets forth the purpose of counterintelligence. It is not an operational guideline except in the broadest sense, and its wording gives the government many options in deciding what constitutes acceptable, permissible, and feasible counterintelligence functions and activities.

The option the government chooses thus represents a political decision based on: (1) its perception of threats to national security and domestic tranquility; (2) legal restrictions; (3) the availability of resources; and (4) domestic political considerations. The decision should be based on the assumption of responsibility for the long-term national interest, as well as current requirements, and it should follow an objective determination of (1) why we need counterintelligence; (2) the role of counterintelligence in the national intelligence system; (3) the responsibilities and functions which constitute a national counterintelligence program; and (4) the organizational and coordinating framework necessary to implement a true counterintelligence program. Thus the door would be open to establishing either a narrowly focused, severely proscribed, and decentralized counterintelligence mechanism such as the US has had for a decade, or to a comprehensive, centralized, coordinated, and well-focused counter-intelligence program.

Counterintelligence in Perspective

Although counterintelligence is concerned with the hostile activities of all foreign intelligence and security services, and all individuals and groups which pose a threat to US internal security, its primary reason for existence is the Soviet Union. To understand fully what counterintelligence is expected to accomplish, it must be understood and kept in mind at all times that the KGB directs all Soviet bloc intelligence services, sustains the Soviet system, and implements a major portion of Soviet strategy throughout the world. The Soviet designation of the US in 1959 as the "main enemy" was, and remains, a deadly serious identification of how the Soviets actually look at the US, and as such it must be recognized that our primary intelligence concern is to know what *our* "main enemy" is doing and planning. The only intelligence function which directly counters the KGB is counterintelligence, and only a comprehensive and true counterintelligence program can cope with the Soviet or any other serious foreign intelligence threat.

Within the national intelligence system, moreover, counterintelligence is the base, the tap root, which nourishes the rest. A nation which lacks a solid counterintelligence program is not only vulnerable to espionage and subversion, but also suffers weaknessees in its intelligence collection and estimative product. The lack of counter-intelligence information helps distort political, military, and economic perceptions and assessments. Foreign policy decisions and actions and related domestic considerations made without the benefit of counterintelligence information and analysis usually lack perspective, as does an over-reliance on technical intelligence unleavened by information from human sources.

This is not overstated. Effective national counterintelligence, whether the product of one agency or, as in the US, several agencies, departments, and the military services, must produce information about our foreign and domestic adversaries which adds dimension to policy considerations and permits us better to see, assess, and neutralize threats to our freedom. Good counterintelligence information can contribute to the interpretation and analysis of the clandestine and scientific intelligence product, and help us to plan more realistic covert action. Counterintelligence information and analysis can also help reassure analysts that the collection process is not tainted by deception or disinformation. Counterintelligence operations provide access and channels through which national strategy and tactics can be advanced, and another window through which to gauge foreign intentions.

In any counterintelligence program, the primary function is to build effective counterespionage in order to ensure that national secrets are safe and our institutions free from foreign penetration or subversion. But this cannot be undertaken in a vacuum. There is an inextricable informational and guidance relationship among all the counterintelligence functions. This means that no aspect of counterintelligence can be succcessful if functions are fragmented, poorly coordinated, or isolated from the very programs they are supposed to protect and support. For example, the recently expanded FBI programs to investigate Soviet disinformation, sensitize American scientists and technological leaders about Soviet methods and techniques, and combat Soviet penetration activities in the US with the aid of the Foreign Counterintelligence System (FCIS) (a computer tracking of the movements and associations of foreign spies and terrorists), although essential, will be limited in effect unless they are compatible and integrated with centralized international counterintelligence programs.

Seeing Counterintelligence as a Whole

Put another way, because the concept seems to be peculiarly elusive, true counterintelligence is the art of examining from a central vantage point the entire spectrum of hostile intelligence activity in the context of our adversaries' intelligence and political strategy, our own national objectives, and the performance of our own and allied intelligence and counterintelligence services—all for the purpose of devising better means of advancing our policies and protecting our nation from espionage, subversion, disinformation and deception, and adverse military, political, and economic action.

A truly centralized counterintelligence system or capability must be aimed at three objectives:

- To gather continually from every available source, overt and covert, detailed knowledge about every foreign intelligence and security service activity—concentrating, of course, on hostile services and their efforts to penetrate and influence our institutions,

- To research centrally, analyze, and disseminate this knowledge, including estimates of the hostile service threat and future activities; and
- To develop the investigative intelligence collection, operational, and security resources to exploit our adversary's vulnerabilities and neutralize his activities against us.

Unless this focus on the fundamental objectives remains constant over a long period of time, the system cannot be made to work effectively. Assuming such constancy, then a good counterintelligence system must encompass five disciplines:

- Knowledge of hostile foreign intelligence and security services;
- Security and proper compartmentation of the counterintelligence and intelligence components;
- Ability to conduct centralized research and analysis of counterintelligence information;
- Possession of resources to conduct investigations and operations; and
- A comprehensive training program in which selected personnel learn the fundamentals and subsequently acquire additional skills.

True counterintelligence is a discipline in itself that must concentrate always on its basic responsibilities. It must be monolithically centralized and apolitical. It must provide balanced, objective appraisals. It must be geared to long-term goals, although quick to seize immediate advantage. It must be guided by national, not individual or agency, policy direction.

There are eleven basic counterintelligence functions that any centralized counterintelligence organization or system must perform:

1. It must conduct research and analysis based on hundreds of case histories, on information from sensitive sources and defectors, on current and past counterintelligence and intelligence collection operations, on overt information, and on information from allied foreign services.

2. It must review and advise concerning the operational security of human, scientific, and technical clandestine intelligence collection and covert action operations. And it must also

coordinate the *bona fides* assessment and processing of defectors from foreign intelligence services.

3. It must initiate and conduct counterintelligence operations and investigations to protect the US from foreign penetration.

4. It must support the counterintelligence activities and the security programs of other US agencies and the military services.

5. It must conduct and support double agent operations.

6. It must support and undertake directed deception operations.

7. It must conduct counterintelligence liaison with foreign services.

8. It must provide counterintelligence analysis, assessments, and estimates about foreign intelligence and security service functions and activities, including those supporting political, economic, military, and disinformation objectives.

9. It must participate directly in the establishment of operational assets for both counterintelligence and intelligence collection overseas.

10. It must conduct and support sensitive counterintelligence investigations and operations, and exploit foreign intelligence service defectors who have knowledge of penetration. And lastly,

11. It must establish good reporting and dissemination mechanisms.

The prerequisite for any good counterintelligence organization is a record system—informational and operational files, name and subject indices, and the ability to retrieve information rapidly. There must be a secure, compartmented, and controlled central record facility regularly and routinely supported by and, on a need-to-know basis, accessible to the entire intelligence community. A central record facility is the indispensable core of the counterintelligence system. It is the depository for knowledge of foreign intelligence services, and serves as the base for threat assessments, investigative and operational planning and guidance, assessments of information and the *bona fides* of agents and defectors, and as a means of evaluating the effectiveness of security programs. A counterintelligence system is only as good as its central record facility.

The complex of counterintelligence objectives, disciplines, and functions, when coupled with the new definition would provide the framework or "yardsticks" for judging the effectiveness of the system on the basis of net results. Not every counterintelligence component would be charged with all of the functional responsibilities. The appropriate breakdown could be determined at the NSC level. Then, assuming the existence of a central body responsible for coordinating and supporting a national effort in counterintelligence and possibly clandestine collection, requirements could be drawn up and assigned by the latter with due regard, of course, for the chartered responsibilities of each CI agency or component. In this way the assignment of functional responsibilities would lead to the levying of operational guidelines both general and specific for each agency in a complementary manner, designed to avoid duplication while respecting the agencies' internal and external obligations. There would be no need to specify the myriad activities and sub-functions which constitute the composite program.

The day-to-day activities, investigations, operations, research, liaison, record management, programming, coordination, and security reviews which vary from agency to agency according to the threats and opportunities to exploit enemy vulnerabilities, can be evaluated on a continuing basis by each agency against the "yardsticks." Detailed "outside" evaluation of the specific activities by the NSC and the President's Foreign Intelligence Advisory Board (PFIAB) would be necessary only if objectives were not being reached or there were weaknesses in the disciplines indicating that certain functions were not being performed satisfactorily. This would also make it clear why the US needs a centralized national counterintelligence system and would indicate some of the governmental action necessary to establish such a system. Promulgation of the objectives, disciplines, and functions would accompany or follow the definition of counterintelligence suggested above.

Toward a National Program

The purpose of a centralized national counterintelligence program would be to integrate, promote, improve, and coordinate the operations, investigations, and research of each counterintelligence agency. This means providing substantive interagency support for all counterintelligence activities, and designating focal points for planning, coordination, and action, plus a comprehensive overview of threats such as terrorism, an inextricably counterintelligence problem, which cross agency responsibilities and international boundaries. In this way we would improve the security of our institutions and our collection programs, add dimension to assessments and estimates, and increase our covert action potential.

Beginning in 1954, and for some 19 years thereafter, the US had within the CIA a centralized counterintelligence component, the CI Staff, which saw a national counterintelligence program as its goal and attempted to attain the objectives, enforce the disciplines, and perform the functions outlined above. Unfortunately, this effort was not bolstered by definitive NSC policy statements or guidelines with sufficient authority to assign intra- and inter-departmental responsibilities leading ultimately toward a true national program, or even to prevent unilateral decisions or actions by individual counterintelligence components or their parent intelligence agencies which might violate or destroy the foundation of centralized counterintelligence.

In the opinion of this observer, the decentralization of CIA counterintelligence in 1973 was a tremendous leap backward in intelligence time. Not only was the intelligence community and public perception of counterintelligence changed, but the dispersal of responsibilities and functions destroyed the one component in the intelligence community where there was a research and analytical overview of the communist world, its parties and its intelligence and security services, and an overview of the counterintelligence problems facing the West, combined with oversight and the initiation of plans and operations designed to combat communist threats to our security. The community lost the ability to assess centrally the significance of and the interrelationships between activities in the international communist movement, Soviet Bloc intelligence services, terrorists, front groups, spies, and the reliability of our sources of information, and to relate this assessment to domestic or internal security problems in conjunction with the FBI. Subsequently, of course, the FBI lost much of its own ability to view the problem of political subversion, terrorism, and espionage contextually with international Soviet Bloc machinations.

The US needs to restore, and then increase, the central counterintelligence capabilities lost in 1973. The logical and efficient way to do this is to reconstitute functional centralized counterintelligence within CIA; the core of a national counterintelligence program should be an organic element in the nation's primary intelligence agency.

CIA in a Pivotal Role

It is important, however, if the US is to have a true counterintelligence program, that, in contrast to the pre-1973 situation, organizational authorities establishing a central counterintelligence component ensure two-way access at the working level between counterintelligence and all other CIA components. Their working relationship must incorporate the following:

- Operational planning, information evaluation, and security review, governed by appropriate security and compartmentation procedures, between counterintelligence and human and technical clandestine collectors, covert action officers, and intelligence analysts and estimators.

- CIA responsibility for services of common concern and for the coordination of intelligence and counterintelligence overseas, which means that the core of the national system should integrate counterintelligence records with other principal intelligence records, and that there must be close coordination in Washington and overseas of liaison between US counterintelligence agencies and allied foreign services.

- CIA possession of operational, doctrinal, and case history archives, in many instances related to CIA's central records and operational activities, which would facilitate the reconstitution of basic files, the creation of new files, and the all-important attempt to incorporate file information not centralized for ten years.

- Recentralization of functions and resources which would provide a base of current operational, investigative, informational security program, and liaison knowledge which can be assimilated for planning and guidance in order to make maximum use of resources in place or with potential to work toward new objectives.

- Combining the CIA's counterintelligence resources and facilitating mutual access between counterintelligence and other CIA components and both US and allied foreign services, whereby the US will gain a much better ability to see the worldwide foreign intelligence threat in realistic perspective and relate this to supporting the activities of all agencies responsible for protecting the nation from espionage and other threats to domestic

tranquility, intelligence collection and foreign policy considerations.

The reasons for constructing a centralized, national counterintelligence program structure would seem to be obvious. The US needs
a first rate intelligence system because for 65 years the Soviets have
been telling us, and demonstrating with increasing efficacy by their
political, military, economic, and intelligence strategy and tactics,
that they are dedicated to defeating us, that they are indeed our
enemies. It should be a simple matter to accept the documented
evidence, assess the actual scope and intensity of the threat, conclude
that the Soviets mean what they say and do, and decide that a
comprehensive counterintelligence program is essential.

But the matter is not that simple. A move toward a centralized
counterintelligence system will create controversy in the mind of the
public and within the government, including the intelligence community. The Executive would have to act assertively to dispel the
confusion, misunderstandings, and ignorance concerning counterintelligence and to give assurance that counterintelligence activities
will be undertaken to protect, not endanger, American freedoms and
civil rights. A basis for this, little noted by the media, was authori-
tatively laid down by Attorney General William French Smith when
he spoke to the Los Angeles World Affairs Council on December 18,
1981, and emphasized, inter alia, that intelligence will be conducted
in a lawful manner with strict accountability and obedience to law.

It is axiomatic that we need good counterintelligence to protect
our civil liberties and freedom, but it is equally true that under our
system of government we cannot have a first-rate counterintelligence
system if we fail to safeguard essential civil liberties. It should also
be noted that there is a point of compromise where, for the good of
the nation, it may be necessary to temper the unbridled exercise of
these rights and establish legally controlled methods of monitoring
and neutralizing actions which jeopardize national interests.

No Threat to Civil Liberties

It is beyond the scope of this paper to attempt to address any of
the legal and civil rights considerations fundamental to the conduct
of counterintelligence in the US. However, it must be noted that,
except as viewed by the radical civil rights activists and the anti-
intelligence lobby, the nation is already moving toward a more

reasonable and rational approach to balancing legitimate concern for civil rights with intelligence requirements. A most encouraging aspect of this move is the fact that a nongovernmental body, the Standing Committee on Law and National Security of the American Bar Association, has expressed its concern while trying to ensure that both American freedoms and national security are protected. The importance of interplay between a responsible nongovernmental body and the government on legal issues involving civil rights and intelligence cannot be minimized, and can only bolster the government's efforts to establish an effective intelligence system. This is highlighted by the remarks of Morris I. Leibman made on the occasion of his retirement as chairman of the Committee:

> One of our most important contributions has been to identify a new body of law called national security law. It began with the recognition that there is a real external threat to our free society. The challenge was to take steps to protect our society without destroying the essential nature of our institutions. This was particularly within the competence and responsibility of the American legal community.
>
> A professor of law, who attended one of our workshops, stated it well in a recent letter to me. He wrote: "The law of national security is that body of jurisprudence, legislation, and judicial decisions which define the actions a State may take in order to protect its vital institutions, interests, and security, against both domestic and external challenges . . . Despite the controversial background of national security legislation in this country, the need for protection of our fundamental institutions cannot be denied.

The process of convincing the intelligence community, particularly the CIA, of the need for centralized counterintelligence may not be easy. The issues, circumstances, and conditions, which underlay the decision to decentralize counterintelligence within CIA have created confusion, misunderstanding, and prejudice. Since 1973, the counterintelligence community has not been concerned about true, national counterintelligence program considerations primarily because there has not been a basis for objective comparison between such a program and the current pattern of counterintelligence activity. It is hard to change an organizational structure and an entrenched bureaucracy after 10 years, and to institute new responsibilities and functions especially if there are insufficient trained and experienced personnel. There is also the residual suspicion that centralized counterintelligence within CIA was somehow responsible for or involved in activities which were not only dangerous but prejudicial to other intelligence activities—specifically, clandestine collection operations.

Decentralization also conveyed an implication to the intelligence community and the public that if the CIA, charged with the responsibility of supporting, coordinating and guiding the US counterintelligence community, had effectively abandoned this service of common concern, then the foreign intelligence threat did not warrant a truly comprehensive counterintelligence program, and that dispersed functions and activities in the CIA and the intelligence community would suffice.

The Threat Defined

Recently, the most crucial issue in terms of national defense, which was a contributing factor in the decision to decentralize CIA counterintelligence, was put publicly in proper perspective by William J. Casey, Director of Central Intelligence. Casey, speaking on August 24, 1982, at the 64th Annual Convention of the American Legion, made an important statement about US intelligence, which included three points quoted below stressing the Soviet intelligence threat. This occurred almost exactly nine years after CIA management rejected a counterintelligence threat assessment which contained these points and others, in documented detail, calling them exaggerated, alarmist, and likely to inhibit the development of intelligence collection and other activities. These three statements, and certainly the information backing up their assessment of the threat, provide a basis for implementing a comprehensive counterintelligence program. A fourth point made by Casey, also quoted, underscores the reasons outlined above as to why the nation needs a true counterintelligence program, tap root of the intelligence system—namely, that counterintelligence analysis, estimates, and threat assessments provide another dimension to intelligence estimates which make it difficult to manipulate intelligence to support preconceived policy decisions or plans—that is to say, for the intelligence community to become a part of policy and political advocacy as happened in 1973.

Mr. Casey stated:

> Still less widely recognized is the Soviet ability and will to project its power worldwide through subversion and insurgency and the adept use of proxy forces, arms sales, and thousands of military advisors scattered around the world . . .

> Now there are still more subtle and less widely understood threats. One is the monster known as international terrorism. The Soviet Union has

provided funding and support for terrorist operations via Eastern Europe and its client nations like Libya and Cuba. With at least tacit Soviet approval, many terrorist groups have trained together in Cuba, Libya, Iraq, South Yemen, Lebanon, and the countries of Eastern Europe . . .

Another threat is the ability of the Soviet Union, largely through its intelligence arm, the KGB, to insidiously insert its policy views into the political dialogue in the United States and other foreign countries. The KGB is adept at doing this in a way that hides the Soviet hand as the instigator . . .

My highest responsibility as Director of Central Intelligence is to produce sound national intelligence estimates on issues relevant to our national security. We've taken steps to assure standards of integrity and objectivity, relevance and timeliness, accuracy and independence in these intelligence assessments . . .

These Casey statements concerning the scope of Soviet intelligence activities in effect call for a centralized overview based on detailed study, and for coordinated, guided investigations and operations to neutralize the Soviet effort. To this might be added the basic assessment of the KGB—also unacceptable in 1973—namely, that the KGB, *in extenso,* is not the intelligence service Americans want it to be. It is not just a spy-counter-spy agency. It is not a mirror image of the US system, and cannot be understood if viewed as though it were. It is a cohesive, vital, integrated element in the Soviet system, and as such plays a prominent role in the formulation and implementation of Soviet policy, including the use of disinformation and deception. The evidence was clear, long before 1973, that since May 1959 the KGB had followed the Politburo injunction to increase its penetration and technological espionage efforts against the "main enemy," in accordance with the December 1958, CPSU and world communism decision (20th World Congress of Communist Parties) to rededicate the communist movement to the principles of Leninism. The 1982 accession of Yuri Andropov to Soviet leadership, after 15 years as KGB chief, highlights the role the KGB has played in Soviet policy.

It would seem that the evidence which prompted the Director of Central Intelligence to make public reference to the scope of the Soviet intelligence threat would have stimulated the government to seek to improve *all* aspects of US counterintelligence. Soviet machinations since Andropov came to power point sharply at this need. In West European political dialogues involving Western defense and political alignments, Soviet intrusions have approached blatant intervention, as they have attempted to influence independent idealistic popular movements. The seeds of espionage, subversion, and disinformation planted by the Soviets over decades now are flourishing because they have been carefully watered and tilled, while the West—especially the US—has abandoned its efforts to uproot or smother the weeds. The Russian thistle cannot be eradicated unless all the "farmers" in the counterintelligence community act in concert, sharing and supporting the collective effort.

It certainly is not now, nor was it in the past, an easy task to build a comprehensive counterintelligence capability. It is especially difficult after a decade of disarray in the counterintelligence community amid contending and contentious views about counterintelligence, reflecting both executive and congressional attitudes. It requires a mustering of political will, notably lacking since at least 1975, for the executive to exercise its responsibility and authority to formulate and implement a national counterintelligence program. There must be a determination to establish objectives, allocate responsibilities, functions and resources, and make organizational and functional changes which transcend individual agency interests. Most important, the executive must establish realistic legal guidelines for the conduct of counterintelligence activities which will advance, not limit, national counterintelligence capabilities.

The program formulated must dispel the confusion and misunderstanding about counterintellience among reasonable people. The test of the Executive's resolve to enhance national counterintelligence capabilities, to cope with the acknowledged danger, will be its willingness to establish a program, explain why the program is needed and what it will do for the nation, and then hold firm to its program despite the clamor of anti-intelligence elements which will gain media and, perhaps again, congressional support.

The Emergence of "Domestic Intelligence"

A primary point of confusion—and inevitably a major issue—is the question of which counterintelligence activities are justifiably necessary within the US and against US persons both within the US and overseas. The government has permitted consideration, if not the solution, of this problem to become lost in the maze of what has become known as "domestic intelligence."

Although the term "domestic intelligence" seems to have become part of the jargon, it makes very little sense unless used to distinguish or categorize information—for example, as foreign intelligence is separated into political, economic, military, and counterintelligence categories. Thus, if used only to identify information concerning threats to internal security or domestic tranquility *which are not instigated or supported by foreign powers,* the term would have a legitimate place in the intelligence lexicon. If used in the latter context, it would mean that domestic intelligence is actually counterintelligence information, although not counterintelligence information as normally defined. If used a bit more broadly, as it might well be, the term might include all information, all intelligence, relating to domestic tranquility and internal security.

Confusion, however, has developed because the term "domestic intelligence" is being used to describe both a locale and a potpourri of activities and information. The latter in turn fall within two distinct but related counterintelligence problems, and one non-counterintelligence problem identified loosely as domestic intelligence because the activity takes place in the US. The primary counterintelligence problem under the umbrella term is straight counterintelligence— protection against foreign threats. As such, it is an integral part of the national counterintelligence effort—what the FBI traditionally termed "Foreign Counterintelligence." The secondary counterintelligence problem involves protection against "home-grown" individuals and groups threatening to subvert our institutions or disrupt domestic tranquility *without* foreign connections or support. The non-counterintelligence problem referred to above includes collection within the US of foreign intelligence (i.e., clandestine collection), or the initiation of activities, likewise within the US, designed to collect foreign intelligence overseas. These undertakings may or may not involve US persons.

"Domestic intelligence" is a pejorative term. It confuses the government, counterintelligence practitioners and, regrettably, even those who understand the need for counterintelligence but are legitimately and sincerely concerned that civil liberties not be jeopardized. The government has fallen into the trap of approaching the problem on terms dictated by opponents of intelligence. The longer the term "domestic intelligence" is used, it will conjure up sinister implications about US counterintelligence. The government will remain on the defensive and reluctant to establish a true counterintelligence program.

The term "domestic intelligence" has unfortunately been accepted in the intelligence community and has taken on a life of its own, similar to the catch-word "destabilize," among the media and opponents of intelligence. It is therefore time for the government to explain what domestic intelligence means in the context of threats to the US within the US and involving US persons which require counterintelligence action or foreign intelligence collection. This would lessen the confusion and establish a rationale for the necessity of certain counterintelligence activities within the US. It would make clear what this involves with respect to civil liberties balanced against threats to those liberties.

This action might well be the most important step the government could take toward establishing a true national counterintelligence program. "Everyone" knows spies have to be caught, terrorism has to be suppressed, and foreigners cannot be permitted to subvert our institutions. What "everyone" does not know are the complexities involved in conducting counterintelligence activities in the US in conformance with the law and guidelines designed to protect civil liberties as well as our freedom.

There are other complexities about counterintelligence which continue to confuse the executive and the counterintelligence community and delay establishment of a national counterintelligence program. The most graphic example is the previously noted separation of departmental security programs from the counterintelligence community's basic functional responsibility to protect our institutions from foreign intelligence penetration—from spies. Another relates to the role and jurisdiction of the central counterintelligence component. The US counterintelligence community is a conglomerate of services, agencies, and components with overlapping, limited, and parochial jurisdictions and functional responsibilities. But these responsibilities derive from the same objectives, disciplines, and functions outlined above as essential to a centralized system.

The Road Toward Centralization

The conglomerate counterintelligence system is a fundamental part of the US system of checks and balances and division of responsibilities which help preserve our liberties and freedoms by limiting the legal, jurisdictional, political, and policy power of law enforcement and intelligence agencies. The system has weaknesses which lead to duplication, contention, certain inefficiencies, and coordination problems, but the basic strengths of the system outweigh the weaknesses. The problem is to establish a centralized program which will draw upon the functional strengths of the conglomerate agencies to enhance the community's overall counterintelligence capabilities while increasing the effectiveness of each agency's functional activities. Properly guided and coordinated, a complementary—even if not fully integrated—system of mutually supporting agencies promotes flexibility in solving problems and exploiting opportunities. It also permits more objective questioning of plans, analyses and estimates, and of course permits focusing multiple resources on investigations and operations.

The centralized counterintelligence component would not be a command agency. It serves as a guidance, coordinating operational and support element for each of the separate intelligence, counterintelligence and security agencies, which would retain their legal and functional jurisdictions and responsibilities while contributing to the same overall objectives. Problems of coordination and cooperation inherent in bureaucracy would remain, but they can be minimized if the central component is properly organized to provide sound guidance, coordination, and support, and is given appropriate direction and authority by the NSC. The latter would act as arbitrator if guidelines and policy decisions fail to cover a point of contention.

It has been suggested that the way to improve counterintelligence is to combine internal and overseas counterintelligence responsibilities and functions in one monolithic super-agency. Even if this were politically and legally acceptable, there are practical problems which would militate against it. An independent counterintelligence agency would only increase the long-standing isolation and separation of counterintelligence from the rest of the intelligence community. A separate agency could not, and should not, have intimate working-level access to other agencies. Nor could it assume responsibility for another agency, much less several agencies with differing responsibilities. All US counterintelligence agencies or components have unique responsibilities to parent agencies. Security and compartmentation requirements essential to any good intelligence system, and indeed to any counterintelligence component, dictate that dissemination of information be controlled on a strict "need-to-know" basis. A "super" counterintelligence agency would compound security problems, and would never obviate the need for counterintelligence capabilities within the FBI, the CIA, or the military services. It would compete for resources, compound the problems of coordination, and add a redundant layer to the bureaucracy.

It may be argued that restoration of centralized counterintelligence in CIA would create the same problems foreseen if an independent counterintelligence agency were to be established. Others might hold that the pre-1973 CIA counterintelligence organization did not produce the necessary results, or that the present system of counterintelligence activities, support, coordination, and research and analysis is effective and sufficient.

Without detailing the reasons why CIA counterintelligence was decentralized, it can be stated that there was a fundamental issue between CIA managers and counterintelligence officers in their perceptions of what a counterintelligence program should do for the nation and for CIA. This difference in perception remains a concern today, and it should be resolved.

No one contends that the pre-1973 CIA counterintelligence organizational structure was ideal, or that it was completely effective and efficient. It was a framework, a base, upon which a national counterintelligence program could have been constructed. It contained the structural components needed to enhance both CIA activities and those of the community because it centralized counterintelligence information and served as a source of knowledge which encompassed doctrine and training, foreign intelligence threat assessments, and coordinated operational and investigative guidance. The important distinction between this and what an independent counterintelligence agency might provide is that CIA's counterintelligence staff was responsible for coordinating and supporting the intelligence community. It had no command or direct operational or investigative involvement outside the CIA.

The structural basis and functional principles upon which CIA's counterintelligence staff attempted prior to 1973 to build a comprehensive national counterintelligence program remain valid, and even more necessary today. They are:

- The fundamental concept that true national security depends upon assurance that our government is free from hostile penetration;

- The need to help sharpen the government's perception of threats to security and stability, and thereby contribute to formulation of foreign policy;
- The need to ensure that clandestine and technical intelligence collection and covert action operations are secure, and that the intelligence product is untaintcd by deception and disinformation;
- The need to undertake counterintelligence operations and investigations—and to support those of other counterintelligence agencies—and to penetrate foreign intelligence services;
- The need to collect, collate, and disseminate counterintelligence information and, as appropriate, other intelligence information;
- The premise that successful counterintelligence and other intelligence activities depend upon security compartmentation, and must be assessed against detailed knowledge of the capabilities of foreign intelligence and security services;
- The understanding that successful counterintelligence operations cannot be run independently of other counterintelligence and intelligence activities;
- The premise that successful counterintelligence must be based on detailed research and analysis, which requires in-depth knowledge of current and historical espionage and other foreign intelligence service activities;
- Recognition that counterintelligence is a profession requiring specialized training, study, experience, and continuity;
- Recognition that counterintelligence activities, and particularly those conducted by CIA, cannot be undertaken independently of national counterintelligence interests and objectives, or the interests and objectives of other agencies;
- The premise that US intelligence—specifically the CIA, which had the most extensive and comprehensive counterintelligence records in the Western world, must exploit this information and support with positive leadership, a national and Western counterintelligence effort; and lastly
- Realization that successful counterintelligence must be a long-term, constantly improving effort designed to reconstruct the mosaic of hostile intelligence activities for exploitation and neutralization; that it cannot be judged realistically by arbitrary

informational or operational production goals, or used as the basis for *ad hoc* partisan analysis or isolated operational decisions.

The US must decide, first of all, whether the foreign intelligence threat is serious enough to justify a first-class counterintelligence program. Then it must decide on the type of program, centralized or decentralized, which will most successfully counter this threat.

CHAPTER FOUR

Covert Action

B. Hugh Tovar

Covert action in the late 1970's showed all the hallmarks of a dying art form. The political and other pressures which brought about that condition seem now to have abated. Yet constraints exist and there is no certainty that the trend of the 1970's has been reversed. This is regrettable. The United States has played the covert action game since we learned to walk as a nation, and may find it necessary to do so again. In the eyes of at least one former practitioner of the art, the time of need is now.

This essay is designed to point out sectors of the international arena where US security is affected, possibly threatened by current developments, and where there may be viable opportunities to influence the course of events to US advantage, using covert mechanisms to supplement diplomatic and other channels. Some of the better known covert action programs of recent decades are then reviewed. Successes and failures among them are noted, and reasons proffered as to why they fared as they did. Against this backdrop there is a suggested framework for the types of covert action that could, and perhaps should, be developed to cope with the problems likely to be with us in the 1980's, plus a generalized indication of the cost levels these approaches might call for. Some of the practical hindrances to effective covert action are discussed and, finally, there is passing commentary on existing public law and draft charter legislation as they bear on US ability to engage in covert action.

Assumptions

To intervene or not to intervene . . . .

The issue is old, and in the polemics of the last ten years intervention has become a very dirty word—something not to be passed over lightly in a discussion of covert action. As a working premise for this inquiry, intervention and its corollary covert action are deemed admissible if their purposes are reasonable, their methods decent, and their results likely to be compatible with public opinion at both the giving and receiving ends.

In this context, where in the world today would intervention be a thinkable proposition? We visualize five major areas where US inter-

71

ests, quite apart from the massive considerations of inflation, energy, population, technology, and the like, which affect the world at large, are specifically threatened:

- Countries of Europe, the Middle East, East Asia, and indeed the US itself where Soviet political action and propaganda are active and aggressive forces.
- Countries of Western Europe, allied to the US, where—if "Eurocommunism" no longer looms quite as threateningly as it did some years ago—the size and strength of the local communist parties are such that their active participation in government is a continuing possibility.
- African and Middle Eastern countries where Islamic radicalism is a potential threat to government stability.
- Less developed countries where emerging nationalism manifests itself in violence and xenophobia, often targetted at the US.
- Any place in the world where terrorism appears, whether as a weapon of nihilistic forces, or, more important, as an instrumentality exploitable by the Soviets and other powers hostile to the US.

Facing these situations, the US today has for all practical purposes concentrated on clandestine collection of intelligence. Covert action seems no longer to figure significantly in the operational posture of CIA. This is a far cry from earlier years when activism was in style and covert action was an important element of this country's response to presumed threats against the national interest. Clearly, times have changed, and the clock is not likely to be turned back.

Does this then exclude covert action as a practical option in future US foreign operations? It need not. A look at the record will show that the US has often displayed great versatility and effectiveness in addressing serious or even critical situations along comparable lines. There are lessons to be learned in both the successes and failures which thus resulted.

The Ingredients of Success

Opinions differ on which, if any, of the Central Intelligence Agency's better known covert action programs were successful. Some were, and the views offered below are predicated on that conviction.

Policy, leadership, and continuity—collectively, these are the *sine qua non* of effective covert action. If policy is an articulation of national interest, the people at the top must first have a sense of it, and they must convey its meaning unequivocally to their subordinates. If the people and the policies change frequently or precipitately, the impetus is lost and confusion reigns. Skillful operators cannot prevail against it. President Truman's good years were 1946-1951, and under his direction major programs were developed in Europe, aimed primarily at forestalling communist political expansion in the democracies of Western Europe. These were positive efforts to enable our allies to cope with their own problems. For example:

- Italian trade unions, press, and political parties, still weak and struggling against their better organized and financed communist counterparts, were given material assistance and professional guidance. Over time, the scope of the programs widened to include a host of activities in the covert psychological realm, targetted directly at the Soviets.
- Paramilitary action in Greece in support of the Truman Doctrine added another dimension to this extensive panoply. Lastly, but overridingly important, the entire effort was conducted against the backdrop of the Marshall Plan and the establishment of the North Atlantic Treaty Organization.

Together, these were an expression of a national commitment to rebuild, revitalize, and sustain Western Europe. Here was policy coordination at its best and biggest, with the State Department, Defense, and CIA marching to the same tune. Somebody in those days was thinking big and thinking comprehensively. The momentum thus generated was powerful enough to carry over into the next administration with no apparent break in continuity.

President Eisenhower's term, 1952-1960, saw the heyday of American covert action and its expansion on three continents. Although the administration had changed, the White House, the Congress, and the public saw international life in essentially the same perspective. Our concern was the global challenge of communism as then visualized, to be confronted whenever and wherever it seemed to threaten our interests. There was also continuity of experience and the professional verve and expertise that went with it. This was particularly true of the CIA. Throughout the fifties, and for some time thereafter, the Agency was dominated by a group of able and effective men who had emerged from the war with a sense of mission and who shared many of the same concerns. (For present purposes this applies primarily to the leadership of the Directorate of Plans (DDP), or Operations as it is called today, and to the senior echelons closely associated with Allen W. Dulles.) Their crusading spirit frequently found a response among similarly oriented officials in the State Department and White House. Coordination of policy and agreement on methods of implementation were thus facilitated, albeit rather informally, to a degree rarely achieved in subsequent years. This happy confluence of men and events shows up vividly in a wide range of covert activity:

- The Philippines, 1952-1956, where the operators did almost everything right, is also a case study in State/CIA collaboration under ambassadorial direction. More important, it showed how an insurgency could be handled without getting the United States directly involved. The untimely death of Ramon Magsaysay in 1957 was regrettable but it had the side effect of ensuring that the operation never turned sour. Official US dealings with Magsaysay were already offering an object lesson in how not to treat a friend. Had he lived longer, we might have ruined him.

- The early CIA spectacular in Iran, 1953, could have no counterpart today. Quite apart from the threat of exposure, which would be great enough to guarantee against such risk-taking, the wheels of policy would probably grind too slowly to permit prompt exploitation of such a target of opportunity. In fleeting moments, such as the Shah's predicament under Mossadegh, conventional diplomacy is rarely able or willing to move quickly enough. On the heels of success, as we learned during the ensuing years, we then face the nagging problem of how to handle a friendly chief of state who is under obligation to us.

- The Guatemala operation in 1954 was noteworthy for reasons quite apart from its tactical success. Compared to covert action in say, Iran or the Philippines, the effort to overthrow Arbenz was large and of high potential visibility. Policy approval and continuing interagency coordination were easy to obtain in the cohesive governmental framework of that day. Nor was there serious danger of leakage by officials who failed to share the enthusiasm of the principles.

Operations during the sixties show a more irregular pattern. The decade began badly with the U-2 incident and the Bay of Pigs. However, once the Kennedy Administration had pulled itself together by early 1962, the message was conveyed to the covert actioneers in no uncertain terms: Where American interests required intervention or counterintervention, intervene we would. The Bay of Pigs was a disaster but it did not mean permanent withdrawal. The following cases illustrate the application of this approach:

- In 1962, when it became apparent that the North Vietnamese in Laos were violating the Geneva Agreement, President Kennedy decided to give clandestine support to elements of the Royal Lao military. CIA carried the main burden. But the Ambassador controlled the program and directed massive participation by other American governmental bodies operating in Laos. At the Washington end, similar mechanisms balanced those in the field. While the policy decisions that evoked and sustained this undertaking remain controversial, it would be hard to match its effectiveness as a coordinated program or its continuity over a turbulent decade.

- There are parallels between Laos and the Congo, 1956-1967. Large-scale paramilitary activity dominated the scene. The Congo program achieved its objective of enabling President Mobutu to impose some stability where chaos had reigned. Nothwithstanding the opportunities for "rogue-elephantry" which the Congo offered CIA, the program was managed under close Washington direction, and in the field the Ambassador called the shots.

- The first phase of covert operations in Chile, 1962-1967, bridged the Kennedy and Johnson administrations without interruption. The bureaucratic consensus which prevailed in the early 1960's, derived from higher authority, made it comparatively easy to maintain effective collaboration among State Department, CIA, and AID participants. Certainly this was the case during the Chilean elections of 1964 and 1965. By 1970, however, the consensus had broken down and the results proved disastrous.

In brief, then successful covert action is predicated on leadership from senior government echelons. It means that people know what they are doing and believe it is right. Continuity is vital. There have to be effective bureaucratic mechanisms to translate these abstractions into controllable programs. Expertise can be developed only through experience. It helps to have it on hand when the need arises.

The Ingredients of Failure

A good place to start looking for the makings of failure is in the successful operation. Weaknesses, unnoticed at first, often show up later. Or times change, and what looked good in one set of circumstances collapses under pressures. Some operations contain built-in guarantees of eventual disaster. Operational failure may also coincide with and quite possibly derive from a deteriorating domestic political environment, national uncertainty, a leadership vacuum, and bureaucratic confusion. Generalizations along these lines are dangerous but worth exploring. If covert action is to have any reasonable chance of succeeding, it must bear a coherent relationship to the main thrust of US foreign policy. Once it transcends the latter's premises or begins to probe the limits of commitment its outlook is dubious.

We have noted above that the years 1948-1951 were fruitful in covert action terms; initial objectives were achieved and operations in Western Europe expanded eastward against the less accessible Soviet and Bloc targets. And yet, while exploiting every trick in the book in the permissive environment of the fifties, we accomplished comparatively little. The explanation seems clear enough today. The Western democracies were allies and their security was traditionally a measure of our own. Covert action was one of the many elements of the national policy apparatus geared to support that premise. In contrast, did anybody know how far we were willing to go in Eastern Europe, or to what lengths we were prepared to push the USSR? If, inconceivably, it had been US policy to use all available means short of war to force the Soviets out of Poland, Hungary, and Czechoslovakia, our use of covert action during the fifties might have been radically different. Instead, and as became strikingly evident in the Hungarian uprising of 1956, US policy was vague and inchoate and contained more than a hint of wishful thinking. Covert action was intensive but inevitably spasmodic, and led nowhere.

The Bay of Pigs episode represents one of the darker periods of both CIA and covert action history. Once described pithily but simplistically as an immaculate failure, it is better viewed as a messy tragedy that should never have been allowed to happen. In the endless post-audits brought to bear upon it, the event emerges successively as a failure of intelligence, a failure of will, a disaster of military planning, or a shambles of execution. There is an element of truth in all of these interpretations.

Was it an intelligence failure? Undoubtedly, and in the grandest sense of the term. It is feckless to argue about guerrilla uprisings or the legion's survival capabilities. They were ancillary considerations at best. The real question developed on the idea that Castro was so shallowly rooted in Cuba that he could be shaken by psychological pressures, as Arbenz had been in Guatemala, and then ousted by a comparative handful of troops. It is easy to visualize the sequence. The concept once conceived, probably at a senior level, is tested on underlings whose instincts and training guarantee an immediate can-do response. Momentum develops rapidly. Conceptualizing is superseded by planning. Policy emerges in high secrecy and, before anyone realizes it, the project is a living, pulsating, snorting entity with a dynamic of its own. Scrutiny by a disinterested body is all but out of the question under such conditions. The people at the top get the answers they want.

Once astride the tiger, options narrow and will becomes a factor in survival. The Bay of Pigs invasion, whether we like it or not in the comfort of hindsight, was based on a plan. Certain things were supposed to happen in a given sequence, which was presumably understood by those in the chain of command. When the plan was interrupted at a critical point (as in the last-minute decision to reduce by half the size of the initial bombing strike against Cuban air targets) by the President on the advice of non-military advisors, we are constrained to question at least his judgment if not his will. And, given the totality of the ultimate disaster, one can only wonder if US naval air strikes could have made the situation any worse.

A simpler and less emotionally-charged case that can still teach us a few lessons is the Indonesian uprising of 1957-1958. The operational specifics are immaterial. In essence, it was an intelligence failure of massive proportions, a total misreading of the Indonesian scene and of the meaning of Indonesian political developments since independence. How did it happen? Washington, that is a handful of key figures in State and CIA, made its own appraisal of events without consulting anyone who knew Indonesia. Rarely has compartmentation been so rigidly enforced. Command and control remained in

Washington. The Mission in Jakarta, including its CIA components, was excluded from all but the most peripheral involvement.

We have noted that even successful covert action may contain the seeds of its own eventual destruction. This is not an argument for no covert action. It raises questions, however, that require consideration before undertaking any major operation. If we involve ourselves in the survival of a chief of state, as we did in Iran in 1953 and on other occasions during the 1960's, we may find it difficult or impossible to disengage gracefully. Often we hesitate to look a client state, even a willing one, in the face. Indecision or failure to follow through is likely to undermine whatever initial success may have been achieved. The question is not solely one of opportunity but perhaps even more of responsibility. In either event the tiger analogy continues to hold.

Guatemala in 1954 was operationally successful, an example of what might be called brash technical virtuosity. But was the game worth the candle? We played into the endemic pattern of Latin American history, military ouster of objectionable civilian governments. Our success was short-lived. It is difficult not to wonder if the planners had read the history of the region before plunging in.

Even continuity when we achieve it may in time plague us. One of the major elements of our covert political action in Europe and elsewhere in the fifties involved international organizations—labor, veterans, women, youth, and students, most of them quite successful in their fields. Weaknesses existed, however, and ramified steadily over the years, primarily in funding procedures which became labyrinthine, cumbersome, and increasingly insecure owing to their reliance on foundations. The *Ramparts* exposures of 1967 marked the end of an era and pointed up our failure to realize that times had changed; what had been acceptable in the fifties became anathema in the late sixties—specifically, the secret use of the nation's private voluntary, religious, or educational organizations.

Laos (1962-1973) cited above as an example of successful management, was also remarkable for its tactical and operational success against a backdrop of strategic failure. Much more important as a lesson for the future, and one that far transcends the issue of whether or not CIA should undertake large-scale paramilitary operations, was our failure to recognize that we were pushing people beyond their limits: the irresponsibility of the strong partner toward the weaker one, particularly when the linkage between their interests and ours had begun to grow tenuous. Following the ceasefire agreement with North Vietnam in February, 1973, Laos was for all practical purposes cast adrift under conditions which virtually guaranteed eventual Communist dominance.

If a government convinced of the worthiness of its causes can both overplay and fail to exploit its successes, one divided against itself cannot engage in rational covert action at all. Chile, 1970-1973, stands as an object lesson in how not to do things. However arguable the case for covert action might have been at the time, the combination of a demanding White House, a strongly opposed State Department, and a CIA leadership that saw fit not to question orders, seems in retrospect to have been an assured loser.

On balance then, failure in covert action may have its roots in the same matrix of energy and effort that promotes success. It occurs when responsible people fail to look far enough ahead and assess the likely consequences of their decisions, or when they vacillate in accepting the sequential relationship with the entities they may have created. If there is a prime factor in the pattern which is certain to bring on trouble, it is excessive compartmentation among decision-makers, planners, and operatives, particularly in the early stages of development. Bad intelligence guarantees bad covert action, which often leads to disaster.

The 1980's: A Framework for Action

Covert action, clearly, is feasible only if we possess the means. In loose intelligence parlance, means are usually described as assets, and they include both sources of information and channels of influence.

Clandestine operations are activities conducted in secret by an intelligence service. They encompass collection of intelligence, counterintelligence, and covert action. Here, the term covert, though synonymous with clandestine, describes an activity or event which generally occurs in the public domain, observable by those who happen to be at hand. It has an identifiable instigator or sponsor, and its covertness lies in the relationship between the latter and some hidden, unacknowledged authority, or source of assistance. Covert action for present purposes thus entails activity in which the US Government's involvement is deliberately concealed. Its aim is to get something done in ways which are compatible with US interests, or which are perhaps directly serving US interests. As a rule—and in fact almost invariably—the action is believed by those who carry it out to be compatible also with their interests. We are thus taking sides in local issues, i.e., intervening in a manner which infringes on host country sovereignty. In such circumstances it is not likely that a covert action asset would be asked or induced, certainly not forced, to do something he did not wish to do. Covert actioneers are in effect the "do-gooders" of the clandestine business, and their stock-in-trade is not seduction and manipulation of innocents, but the *sub-rosa* support and succor of peoples and institutions legitimately in need of such assistance. Many honest intelligence officers think this is a waste of time and effort. So do many US ambassadors.

These attitudes are regrettable, the more so because they often entail misunderstanding of the activity in question. Covert action need not—indeed, rarely does—involve direct pressure on a government aimed at bringing it down or drastically changing its behavior. It is much more likely to entail exertion of influence on a government through its regular constituencies, to persuade it to follow a course of action supported by many if not all, local leaders. The individual pressure points may be our agents or witting collaborators, but they are accountable for their actions to those they represent, and are usually just as anxious as we are to protect the existence of their covert association and any suggestion of financial support.

The purpose of the latter may be to permit the individual to carry on his public life with a modicum of financial security, or it may be to strengthen the organization he represents and enable it to play its role more effectively in the local political milieu. Conversely, there may be no agent relationship involved at all, nor material support of any kind. The association may be discreet without being clandestine, and may devolve on the exchange of ideas and guidance, or advice.

Covert action involving media is almost invariably targetted at getting good information—the facts, the truth—into print, sometimes on the air, under conditions where without our intrusion it would not appear. In less developed countries journalists often have trouble obtaining usable material on broad issues or international problems, and may welcome assistance. If this sometimes results in a clandestine salaried relationship, it does not entail a stranglehold on the newspaper or saturation of the market with propaganda. More often than not, the immediate purpose is local play or replay of solid news material or intelligent commentary on subjects of international or even local interest. It is rare that a "black" or otherwise sinister piece emerges in such a context. Covert action thus encompasses a very wide spectrum of activity. It is most effective when conducted in close coordination with the overt programs of government under direction of the Ambassador.

If, from the standpoint of what Americans perceive as right and licit, these clandestine interventions can ever be justified, we suggest that it is in the context of the threats to our security outlined in the opening paragraphs of this paper. What, for example, are the Soviets doing in countries where they see an opportunity to further their own interest? Excluding for the moment the truly "hot" areas like Angola, South Yemen, and Ethiopia where the Soviets have deployed their Cuban paramilitary assets, or Afghanistan where they have intervened directly and massively with regular military forces, we can point to:

- Japan, where they are massively engaged in building a base of influence as well as intelligence collection, aimed at counterbalancing the US presence and developing a foil against political and economic intrusions of the People's Republic of China (PRC)

- Important countries such as Indonesia, where they are trying to capitalize upon a latent but not necessarily dormant communist movement, to acquire friends and assets in the press, the political parties such as they are, and the government itself

- Countries such as Thailand, which feel threatened by the PRC, where the Soviets are cultivating a benign image of their own while buying assets in the media and in government and commercial circles

- Western Europe where the Soviets not long ago mounted a massive and very successful propaganda attack against the enhanced radiation weapon, with significant impact on US defense policy and relations with our European allies, and where today they have a hand in the spreading peace movement

- The United States where the Soviet official presence, already overloaded with intelligence personnel, pursues its clandestine objectives with minimal interference, and is not greatly affected by the charges of Senator Moynihan that the Mission is engaged in an enormous electronic intercept operation within the nation's capital.

Given resource limitations and the vast spread of US interests, it would be difficult and costly to match the Soviet effort across the board. (The CIA estimates them at $2-3 billion per year.) But we could do much more than we are today without seriously damaging the larger framework of US-Soviet relations. One way would be to strengthen our techniques for speaking directly to the peoples of the Soviet Union. Instead of only lamenting violations of human rights, we could find new ways to encourage dissident elements both directly and indirectly.

We might also figure out how to get at the peoples of Eastern Europe, to induce greater independence of thought and resentment of their subordination to the Soviets. If there is any doubt that the Soviets are susceptible to such pressures, it can be dispelled by a look at the successes and history of Radio Free Europe and Radio Liberty. Today, though divorced from CIA, both radios continue to infuriate the Soviets. And surely the continuing Polish crisis demonstrates how vulnerable the Soviets are even within their own power sphere.

It is not permature to assess the People's Republic of China in similar terms. The 1978 attack on the Socialist Republic of Vietnam shows how far the Chinese may be prepared to risk their new image in situations they consider vital. By the same token, both the Chinese and Vietnamese are vulnerable to pressure we have hardly considered to date. As official relations with China and Vietnam develop, we should examine ways to exploit their differences, including the use of covert action channels not yet in existence. In Third World countries, we must decide where our interests are critically affected, and that done, concentrate systematically on neutralizing both Soviet and Chinese operations there. This means identifying them, then using covert channels to blunt their effectiveness.

If the mind boggles at communist parties in France, Italy, Portugal, or Spain playing key roles in government, the obvious question is whether the US should act to forestall it, or merely stand aside and record the trend. If the latter, we can relax, but not for long. The alternative would be prompt action to find out what is going on within the communist parties. This requires responsive sources within the communist ranks. It also means laying the foundations for covert action by:

- Developing contacts within key pressure groups—labor, students, women, professionals, etc.—which are certain to be drawn toward coalition (or competition) with communist-dominated fronts

- Acquiring independent contacts within the local media who can expose the clandestine maneuvering of the communists and progagandize on behalf of democratic government free of communist intrusion

- Staying in discreet touch with various levels of the body politic sympathetic to US interests, which might be in need of material support or political advice

- Attempting to split the communist parties on ideological or political issues which entail internal cleavages

- Using our leverage on the communist parties to pressure the Soviets.

Though large subsidies once figured prominently in the US covert action arsenal, they would not be needed in today's Western European political milieu.

It is hard for Americans to fathom the turbulent swell of Islamic radicalism and its seemingly mindless violence. We are stunned when friendly governments are suddenly engulfed and overthrown in explosive outbreaks that seem to be beyond our ability to influence or modulate. Yet, we have dealt successfully with such situations—specifically, in Iran in 1953. The method parallels that suggested for dealing with communist parties:

- Acquiring intelligence, notwithstanding the host government's desire to limit our access

- Developing responsive contacts in all important pressure groups, both pro- and anti-government

- Exploiting contacts in both government and opposition not only to influence their behavior when feasible, but also to reflect a posture of disinterestedness that may later facilitate our dealing with a new government
- Utilizing non-official (CIA) channels to supplement official (Department of State) relations with the host government to induce a rational response by the latter to the forces pressuring it.

It is obvious that some of these ingredients were missing in Iran during the period leading up to the overthrow of the Shah's government. If Islamic radicals are hard to cope with, we often fare no better with "normal" nationalist upheavals. Usually we misunderstand them. Without pretending that the US, by remaining flexible and maneuvering cleverly, can avoid becoming the target for some of the emotion and pent-up resentment characterizing such upheavals, the techniques of adjustment and modulation are nonetheless available if we wish to use them. They include:

- Understanding the emerging forces on their own terms: impossible without listening to them and speaking with them
- Ensuring that we have responsive contacts in the nationalist movements who can tell us what is going on, and through whom we can convey whatever messages we may wish to send
- Diversifying our contacts to include access to the movements' constituent pressure groups
- Using our contacts within the host government to influence the latter's response to domestic pressures
- Identifying and ensuring contact with the likely survivors of any prospective upheaval.

A truly gruesome threat to effective implementation of US policy abroad today is terrorism in its varied manifestations. The roster of murdered ambassadors makes this brutally clear, and its extension to include only one CIA station chief to date stands as a minor miracle. If, as a CIA report once put it, "one man's terrorist is another's freedom fighter," and if a Carlos can be trained by the Soviets and then obtain political and logistical support from a Qadhafi in Libya, the threat obviously impinges upon equities that make it difficult to cope with. The sheer physical danger involved in terrorist

suppression complicates it further. Clandestine methods of dealing
with the problem include:

- Penetration of the terrorist organizations and of the political
  entities they purport to represent, to ascertain in advance when
  and where they are going to strike
- Exchanging information and technology with other governments
  facing the terrorist problem
- Exerting all possible influence on interested governments to
  effect systematic and coordinated terrorist suppression programs
- Applying pressure on the Soviets to ensure that they do not
  exploit terrorism for their own purposes, and on lesser states
  such as Libya, to prevent the harboring, training, or support of
  terrorist elements
- Developing a paramilitary force capable of striking hard and
  quickly against terrorist atrocities in the manner of Entebbe and
  Magadiscio.

The key point bearing on most of the above is that if these problems
are to be addressed in the 1980's, the groundwork—the infrastructure, as some call it—must be laid today. It will not spring into being
upon command. This means development of assets, individual and
organizational, at all levels and in key sectors of the societies wherein
we perceive US interests to be potentially threatened. But development is not enough. The mechanisms must be activated and used
carefully and systematically to ensure their vitality in advance of the
day of crisis. Under normal circumstances covert action assets will
also serve as useful, even valuable, sources of information.

Budget and Infrastructure

Another reality to be faced is that US covert action capabilities
were approaching ground-zero as the 1970's closed. Any attempted
projection of needs and costs into the 1980's must therefore be
predicated on creation of new assets, as opposed to utilization of
assets already in being.

We assume that budgetary restraints will continue to inhibit desirable covert action initiatives. Although there have been press reports
suggesting that substantially increased funds for covert action have

been made available to CIA by the present administration, it would be unrealistic to visualize a return to operations on a scale comparable to the 1950's or early 1960's. Those were times, as the Katzenbach Committee disclosures of 1967 made clear, of very large-scale programs. Nor do the late 1960's or early 1970's offer a useful standard of cost comparison. Paramilitary operations dominated the scene then, as in Laos—1965 through early 1973—and budgets were substantial.

On balance, and with apologies for such generalities, we can safety suggest late 1975 as a reasonable point of departure. (The price tags on covert action at that time are not on public record, but the full brunt of efforts to cut covert action had not yet been felt.) Modest as then existing covert action mechanisms probably were, we may assume that not many of them remained viable for long. To propose rebuilding an operational infrastructure along 1975 lines, with allowance for the inroads of inflation, offers something to shoot at. If conditions later call for an expansion of effort, that need not entail "big money." Indeed, we doubt that in this day and age, big money can any longer be moved securely or absorbed effectively by a recipient. Covert action outlays should thus remain limited, catalytic in nature, designed to supplement and stimulate rather than subsidize forces or entities of our choice. A plausible exception to these limitations would of course occur in the event CIA were required to reenter the field of paramilitary operations on a significant scale.

Covert Action Applied

Implementation of covert programs falls largely to CIA stations abroad, and if the latter are as ubiquitous and energetic as often alleged, there should be few problems getting things in motion. However, it does not always work that way. Stations vary widely in composition, target orientation, and effectiveness. Their lack of uniformity derives from the nature of the organization itself. CIA was designed to respond to the orders of the President. Its basic charter, the National Security Act of 1947, is vaguely worded and permits a wide range of activity. This also makes for changing emphases in periods of competing priorities.

There is often disagreement in the Intelligence Community and within CIA itself as to exactly what the Agency should be doing with its manpower and money. Some argue that CIA, specifically the

Operations Directorate, should not collect current intelligence. Others have no use for covert action. Thus stations over the years have tended to shift, or drift, with the winds of policy and internal pressure. Some distinctive patterns, however, have emerged, reflecting reactions at senior levels of government to performance. They leave no doubt that the value of a station has been, and will probably continue to be, measured not only by its ability to provide timely intelligence, but equally in the way it discharges action responsibilities. Over the years, the stations which have distinguished themselves in covert action have generally been those which were well-regarded as collectors of intelligence. In both instances, the key to success has been access to the movers and shakers of a country.

If action capabilities take time to develop, it is also important that, once in being, they be used or they will atrophy. When upper echelons of government are not interested in the march of events in a presumably threatened country, intelligence finds no market, and there is even less interest in covert action. This usually means reallocation of resources and, predictably, trouble later when pressures resurface. To maintain its operational viability in the face of reduced policy-level interest, a station must fend off requirements from CIA Headquarters to do other things, and resistance—often heavy—from the local ambassador who does not wish to see the Agency "stirring up the animals" or encroaching upon the terrain of his political section. Not least of all, it will face personnel shortages. Stations are getting smaller as requirements increase. Under such circumstances it will be more difficult than ever for stations to develop and maintain viable contacts within the power centers of a target country.

Similar constraints will affect efforts on our part to influence events beyond the Iron Curtain or in the realm of international organizations where the Soviets remain exceedingly active. In the United Nations with its ancillary or associated bodies, the Soviet clandestine apparatus is pervasive, and its operatives have a free hand without significant interference or competition from the US.

In the more openly embattled regions where the Soviets now operate vigorously through their Cuban, East German, and Vietnamese proxies, we appear to have developed no effective counterintervention techniques. Thus the Soviets remain at libery to exploit a sector wherein the US once excelled. The US could profitably reconstitute its ability to use force, covertly or otherwise, without commitment of uniformed military personnel. Debates on this issue in recent years have favored the Defense Department as the more plausible locus for such an undertaking. One way or another, a choice should be made, and the decision kept secret. There are strong arguments for placing paramilitary operations under tactical control of CIA, while drawing upon the Department of Defense for manpower and logistics.

Why CIA? Because CIA has the experience under a wider range of conditions than Defense. CIA also has the institutional memory and the organizational flexibility. The US military operates on a grand scale, reducible only with difficulty, and has a harder time keeping things quiet. It has the best available personnel resources, but cannot effectively encourage the specialization necessary in this narrow field. CIA probably has enough paramilitary expertise on hand to collaborate with the military in building a small force which the President could deploy where he sees American interest jeopardized. We have noted Entebbe and Magadiscio as the types of situation where this might occur. Another might be the need to evacuate Americans in the face of an embassy take-over, as occurred in Teheran, or to extract isolated personnel from threatened technical installations. The largest single obstacle to effective use of such a force in a manner approximating secrecy would be transportation. There is unfortunately no Air America available today. While there are ways around this obstacle, they founder on the question of deniability. Short of the latter, "stonewalling" can be a viable alternative if a responsible decision to act has been made at the policy level.

Action in Perspective

Objections to US involvement in covert action come from those who oppose it in principle, and from those who question its efficacy. Our working premise is that it is often necessary, and can be undertaken within normal standards of decency. It can be very effective. This was demonstrated, as we have noted above, in Laos, 1962-1973; the Congo, early 1960's; the Philippines, 1951-1953; Iran, 1953; Western Europe, 1948-1953; and in the performance of Radio Free Europe and Radio Liberty, 1951-1967. The past decade and a half has seen steady erosion of US covert action programs, our heavy commitment to paramilitary activity during the Vietnam war not withstanding. Much of the curtailment stems from exposure and the outright prohibition on certain categories of involvement and association, beginning with Katzenbach, extending through the Rockefeller and later congressional reviews, and culminating in specific legislative decisions backed up by Executive instructions and guidelines. The net effect is that today that CIA has lost its former zest for covert action.

The clock, of course, will not be turned back. Yet some encouraging recent developments suggest grounds for amelioration of a hitherto rather dismal situation. The 1974 Hughes-Ryan Amendment with its onerous requirements for a presidential finding on the importance of national security of each special (non-collection) operation, plus reporting on the same to each of eight interested congressional committees, was rescinded by the Intelligence Oversight Act of 1980. Now, a finding must still be made, but reporting is confined to the two intelligence oversight committees—a far more secure and expeditious procedure. Allowance is also made for reporting in "extraordinary circumstances" only to the Chairmen and Ranking Minority Members of the two intelligence committees. The law also makes it clear that reporting to the intelligence committees is intended to provide the latter with an opportunity for prior comment, not consent.

The Intelligence Identities Protection Act took the process an important step further. If intelligence people appear obsessed with exposure, it stems from a concern that we keep faith with those who cooperate on the expectation that we will protect the relationship. Exposure can often occur without identification by name. The movers and shakers of a country are often few in number and easily spotted. Too close a focus by too many people may expose them as effectively as a deliberate leak. CIA officers have been deeply perturbed at our apparent inability to protect sources and methods, and have long favored enactment of a law imposing civil and criminal sanctions on persons with authorized access to intelligence secrets who wrongfully reveal them. The exposures of the past decade have unquestionably affected the willingness of foreign contacts to collaborate with Agency operatives. It is a wonder they will work with us at all. Exposure through error or even stupidity in the field is a recognized hazard. It is something else, however, to ask for cooperation at possible risk of life when the real danger is exposure through the act of a US Government official or, worse, a disgruntled former Agency employee. While the language of the press may tout these clandestine relationships as based on bribery, subornation, coercion, or trickery, the reality is quite different. People associate themselves with the Agency's activities abroad because they see generally their own interests and those of their homeland advanced in the process. We owe them and ourselves reasonable protection.

With the Intelligence Identities Protection Act now on the books, that is no longer in the realm of wishful thinking. And that the President saw fit again to express his very positive attitude toward intelligence through his presence at CIA Headquarters on the occasion of signing should militate against vestigial negativism in US intelligence circles.

A charter for the intelligence community, given the chaos of the 1970's has struck many observers as essential. The point has been argued pro and con and, though never suggested as a panacea, it seemed to offer a basis for moving ahead. Applied to covert action specifically, one is hard pressed to visualize any viable legislative definition of the conditions under which covert action could or should be undertaken. On the contrary, the attempt might well ensure against covert action ever being undertaken, because no one would care to risk violating the restrictions. The safest action would thus be no action.

It would seem on balance that covert action is adequately founded on Executive authority, buttressed by the National Security Act of 1947 and the Intelligence Oversight Act of 1980. The past few years have brought a needed respite from external pressure on CIA, and a considerable measure of equilibrium seems to have been regained. We have some distance to go before an impact on covert action can be achieved, but the building process ought by now to be well under way. Covert action is a viable technique for furthering our national interests. It has been effective in the past, and it can be again.

CHAPTER FIVE

Reforms and Proposals for Reform

Angelo Codevilla

The American intelligence system has been under fire for the better part of a decade. Proposals for reform have varied from outright abolition, to major restructuring of the community, to smaller changes intended to advance or set back the fortunes of particular groups or programs within the intelligence community. Although a variety of politicians, journalists, and bureaucrats have taken an interest in the field, few have approached it by explicitly setting forth their view of what the United States must do in an increasingly hostile world, and what sort of intelligence the nation needs in order to grapple with that world. Consequently, all too often prescriptions for reforms of our intelligence system have flowed from political or institutional prejudices rather than from reasoned statements of requirements.

Proposed Charter Legislation
In The Late 1970's

By the early 1980's much of the debate which had surrounded the Church Committee's 18 month-long investigation of the CIA's real and alleged wrongdoing had come to an end. A more fundamental discussion about the role of intelligence in the US government was just beginning. This can be discerned in a pair of articles that appeared in the *Wall Street Journal* on February 23, 1979, written by two members of the Senate Intelligence Committee, Walter Huddleston (D-Kentucky) and Malcolm Wallop (R-Wyoming).

Sen. Huddleston was then leading a last-ditch effort to enact legislative charters for the intelligence agencies as originally conceived by the Church Committee. The Charters were also designed to substitute legislative authority for the executive authority that had hitherto been the basis for US intelligence activity.

The Charters proceeded from the Church Committee's judgment that the country was threatened by a surfeit of intelligence capability. They would have authorized specific intelligence activities case-by-case only in circumstances carefully designed to avoid any repetition of the abuses with which the agencies had been charged in the past. Only activities specifically authorized would have been lawful.

Sen. Wallop opposed the Charters claiming that, in most cases, there is no relationship between the quality of intelligence work and the level of intrusion into civil liberties, and that events had demonstrated that the American people are endangered not so much by the agencies' propensities to excess, but by their inability to do their work. Wallop said that the recent mis-estimation of the Soviet strategic build-up, the failure to gather sufficient information about the Shah of Iran's impending fall, various failures in counterintelligence, and the non-existence of any effective capability covertly to influence events abroad should lead the Congress to reform the intelligence community with a view to strengthening its performance. Sen. Huddleston admitted that US intelligence was not performing as well as it should. He insisted that the Charters were meant not to restrict, but rather to authorize specific activities in specific circumstances and therefore to enhance performance.

Sen. Huddleston's argument clearly reflected a shift in position. It meant that the proponents of reform had abandoned their original argument, that US intelligence was more than adequate to its task, and that we suffered from a surfeit of intelligence. The Charters' proponents were then forced to demonstrate that the Charters' "authorizations"—in other words, limitations or restrictions—would improve performance. Because the restrictions were not conceived for that purpose, the case was hard to make. Because the Charters could not be passed on the grounds on which they had been conceived, they would have to be promoted on grounds uncongenial to them.

The Charters' proponents however, had one important asset: the testimony of top officials of the intelligence community that without the Charters the "professionals" would be reluctant to take the initiative, and would henceforth do only what they were told. There was no shortage of high officers willing to make this argument. Between 1976 and 1980 an almost complete turnover had occurred among the several hundred top employees of the intelligence community. By 1980, virtually no senior officers who had been in senior positions prior to the "revolutions" beginning in 1975 remained in place. The new incumbents were well-attuned to the Church Committee's approach. In 1978 their support had been the key to passing the Foreign Intelligence Surveillance Act (FISA), conceived by the same people who drafted the Charters as a means of bridling the Executive Branch's authority to conduct electronic surveillance for purposes of national security. But in 1979 and 1980, during the Charter debate, even the unanimous, strenuous, and heartfelt efforts of these intelligence officials were unpersuasive.

The Congress, for example, did not doubt the assertion of the then Director of the National Security Agency, Admiral Inman, that he and his colleagues would feel on a firmer legal basis were the Charters to pass. Yet the Congress had serious reservations about "purchasing" these professionals' "good will" at the price of a statute which, on its face, did not tell any official to do anything, but instead only mandated voluminous procedures. The professionals' argument that the Charters merely ratified the way the intelligence community had been functioning since 1976, and particularly since President Carter's Executive Order 12036, served unintentionally to strengthen the Charters' opponents.

After all, since 1976 American intelligence often had failed demonstrably. The professionals' arguments did not deal substantively with the question of quality in their own work. These officials did not seem willing to acknowledge that they had made mistakes, or that any improvement might be necessary in the product, processes, organization, or personnel of intelligence. Against this, the Charters' opponents argued that precisely because present performance should be improved, the agencies needed new directions and new leadership. Thus the "professionals' " endorsement of the Charters was devalued.

In the spring of 1980, the last attempt to pass the Church Committee's Charters was abandoned. Instead, the Charter bill's legislation number, S. 2284, became the vehicle for a wholly different bill which repealed the Hughes-Ryan Amendment (which had required the CIA to report each covert action to eight congressional committees.) This bill, the Intelligence Oversight Act of 1980, required that the intelligence community report covert action only to the two intelligence committees, and that it keep them fully and currently informed of all significant intelligence activities, including "intelligence failures." This latter provision is a sign of widening recognition that, in the 1980's, the US stands to suffer more from the intelligence agencies' deficiencies than from their excesses. Thenceforward debate would concentrate on *how* the nation's intelligence requirements for the 1980's might be met.

However, the debate remained lively because the participants continued to promote very different agendas. The progenitors of the

Church Committee and of the Charter proposals sought to entrench the concept of intelligence operations embodied in the Carter executive order and the Foreign Intelligence Surveillance Act, and to prevent the passage of legislation which could marginally undermine that concept, such as modification of the Freedom of Information Act (FOIA). Officials of the intelligence agencies, having embraced the ways to which they had become accustomed since the mid-1970's, also supported legislation to limit FOIA's application to them, as well as other measures, both legislative and administrative, to decrease the amount of knowledge about intelligence in the public domain. Concurrently, officials of each agency supported increases in funds and authority for themselves. Yet a third set of observers, in the Congress and in academic life, while generally supporting increases in the agencies' funds and authority, concentrated on proposals to specify the intelligence agencies' missions and to improve the performance in each of the elements of intelligence.

Thus in the early eighties, as the debate on intelligence continued, career intelligence officers, sometimes supported by the American Civil Liberties Union (ACLU) and former associates of the Church Committee for their own reasons, argued that little if anything should change. Meanwhile, outsiders pointed to insufficiences in objectives, structures, or procedures as arguments for change.

The Republicans in 1980

On July 1, 1980, a group of Republican senators led by Malcolm Wallop (R-Wyoming) and Paul Laxalt (R-Nevada) introduced a pair of charter bills (S. 2928 and S. 2929) based on a critique of the agencies' performance which had first appeared in September 1979 in the Republican National Committee's White Paper on Intelligence. The substance of these proposals was reflected in the national Republican platform for 1980.

These documents envisaged changing the framework inherited from the Church Committee and crystallized in President Carter's executive order for intelligence. Above all, they rejected the latter's concentration on the conditions the agencies must meet in order to initiate activity. Instead, these bills would have provided statements of missions that, among other things, could be used as standards for measuring the agencies' performance.

They also recommended separation of the office of the Director of Central Intelligence, the President's chief adviser on intelligence, from that of the Director of the Central Intelligence Agency. This was designed (1) to remove CIA from politics, and (2) to undo the present anomalous situation in which one of the intelligence community's branches, CIA, exercises *de facto* authority over other operating branches. This recommendation would also have relieved the DCI of the burden of trying to perform three very difficult jobs.

The bills also would have replaced the present system in which all agencies contribute to a single National Intelligence Estimate on any given question, by one in which at least two agencies, working from the same data base, produced independent estimates. A multiplicity of sources, they contended, would provide better quality control, and would expose decision-makers to a range of arguments within the intelligence community.

In the field of collection, they recommended that the basis of the present clandestine service be shifted from officers in shallow official cover, towards officers under deeper cover. The latter would serve longer tours in each area and would be able to operate even during hostilities. Technical systems for collection should also be reconfigured. This would deemphasize the very costly and otherwise unproductive mission of monitoring arms control agreements, while emphasizing better coverage of military objectives in case of hostilities.

In the field of counterintelligence they advocated the establishment of independent career specialities within CIA and FBI, as well as permanent mechanisms of coordination between the many agencies and disciplines of intelligence for purposes of counterintelligence. With respect to covert action, they simply advocated rebuilding the nation's ability covertly to influence events abroad. Finally, they called for the reestablishment of the Preisdent's Foreign Intelligence Advisory Board (PFIAB), which President Carter had abolished. The PFIAB had given the President insights into the intelligence community independent of vested interests within the community.

The Reagan Administration

The Reagan Administration, however, has made few changes in the structure or operation of American intelligence. In December

1981, the Administration produced an executive order on intelligence (EO 12333), which revised the Carter Executive Order without changing its division of responsibilities. Nor did it define responsibilities of each of the community's various parts, or formulate those responsibilities as affirmative missions. Instead, it retained the Carter Order's focus on conditions that must be met in order to trigger various authorizations. However, because the tone of EO 12333 is much more affirmative, sharp questions were raised by some senators as to whether authority for investigations was being significantly expanded. Spokesmen for the intelligence community made it clear that the changes in rhetoric were not meant to result in activities different from those of the recent past. This led other observers to ask why rhetorical changes were made in the first place.

The most substantive change in the Executive Order removed the prohibition against intelligence collection by the CIA in the United States. This was merely to allow the CIA to follow up domestic aspects of foreign cases. Representatives of CIA were reported to have briefed the two congressional intelligence committees on their intentions. None of the members made public any objections. Nevertheless, the provision led legislators and editorialists into a heated controversy over whether the Reagan Administration meant the CIA to "spy" on innocent Americans.

One factor behind this provision was the desire of some at CIA to expand the Agency's powers at the expense of the FBI. However this controversy's principal result was to confront the public with a false question: shall the CIA be given the power to investigate Americans in the US? The more relevant question was not raised: have the intelligence agencies—both FBI and CIA—been given adequate guidance regarding what investigations they will or will not carry out in the public interest? Because of this controversy, in 1982 the national debate concerning intelligence became somewhat reminiscent of the days of the Church Committee, when questions about the uses, effectiveness, and efficiency of intelligence operations were obscured by others concerning the possible harm our own intelligence might do to our civil liberties.

Also in 1982, the Congress passed, and the President signed, the Intelligence Identities Protection Act, which would punish anyone who discloses the identity of any undercover employee of American intelligence, when he does so in the course of a "pattern of activities" which impairs or impedes the intelligence activities of the US. In other words, the Act does not punish anyone in the general public for inadvertent disclosures, or those undertaken in the course of scholarship or in the search for abuses, but only those made as part of a larger pattern of activity which harms American intelligence.

Thus, by the end of 1982, two of the three conditions which many professional intelligence officers had blamed for alleged shortcomings in the agencies' performance, the Hughes-Ryan Amendment and the lack of legal protection for agents' identities, had in the main been corrected by law. The agencies' repeated requests for relief from the Freedom of Information Act did not advance in 1981 and 1982, primarily because the intelligence agencies' managers failed to muster sufficient evidence to support their principal contention, that the existence of FOIA is the main reason why the intelligence services of friendly countries, and potential sources of information, are not cooperating with us as fully as they might. Opponents of relief argued that such non-cooperation may result from other factors, and that the FOIA does not force any agency to release classified information. Thus, they argued, if the agencies have released information they should have protected, and which has frightened away potential collaborators, they have only themselves to blame. During 1982 the Senate Judiciary Committee approved a measure of relief from FOIA so weak that its supporters decided not to push it further, preferring to wait until a better case could be made.

While these developments were under way, the coalition which had succeeded in passing the Foreign Intelligence Surveillance Act (FISA) in 1978 began tentative efforts to make the practice of physical surveillance (shadowing and physical searches) by intelligence agencies subject to the same procedures and same special court mandated by FISA for electronic surveillance. They argued that the agencies should indeed be doing more physical surveillance, but are afraid to do it without a firm legal basis. Opponents contended that it is unconstitutional to make lawful acts by executive agencies subject to prior judicial approval. Those opposed to broadening the scope of FISA argued that the proponents are primarily interested in expanding the application of the "criminal standard" rule, according to which no one way become the object of an intelligence agency's attention unless there is evidence that he has committed or may be about to commit a crime. They maintain that better leadership and changes in personnel, rather than tampering with the law, should be the answer to timidity on the part of intelligence officials. These opponents insist that intelligence and law enforcement are entirely different kinds of activity and cannot be administered under the same regulations.

In 1982 and early 1983 there were also revisions of the guidelines which explain the executive order to working-level intelligence officers, and which govern the conduct of investigations. Before putting them into effect, the Executive Branch discussed the guidelines with the Congressional intelligence committees, assuring the latter that there would be no significant change in the agencies' methods.

The President's Foreign Intelligence Advisory Board (PFIAB) was reestablished in 1981. Like its predecessors, the Board included some persons of great eminence and independence. The new PFIAB, however, was given a larger mission than its predecessors. The new PFIAB, for instance, is expected to bring an element of "competitiveness" into intelligence analysis by doing its own studies of selected topics in current intelligence, and comparing those with the National Estimates. It is also expected to integrate the various intelligence disciplines for a comprehensive look at counterintelligence. It is expected to improve collection, and to provide perspective on covert action. It is far from clear that such a small body of busy, prominent people can do more than carry out the traditional mission of PFIAB to concentrate on quality control. Above all, it is not clear that the President or the DCI will follow the Board's recommendations when they are opposed by the prestige, volume of argument, and bureaucratic skills of senior career intelligence officers. If the President, upon advice of the DCI, refuses on principle to countenance recommendations opposed by the intelligence bureaucracy, this will limit the usefulness of the PFIAB.

In any event, halfway through the Reagan Administration, the laws, organizational arrangements, and basic procedures established by the revolution which the Church Committee and the Carter Administration carried out in the mid-1970's remained in place for all practical purposes.

Proposals For Substantive Reform

In fact, however, the debate did not again revert to what it had been in the early to mid-1970's. First, because the several agencies themselves had become the foremost lobby for restrictions, either in the form of charter legislation or in the form of expansion of the

Foreign Intelligence Surveillance Act. Second, and more important, the record of intelligence failures, the existence of the oversight committees, and the work of independent academics and journalists, have convinced most observers that the agencies may not be able to serve the country as will be required in the 1980's.

Proposals for reform in the field of intelligence, and even from those who would further restrict the agencies, are now likely to be couched in terms of improved performance. On occasion, some in the agencies themselves have grudgingly recognized their own short-comings, or at least have appeared to do so, perhaps out of deference to the President's platform. In sum, a kind of vague consensus has grown up around the idea that the intelligence agencies are not "rogue elephants" but normal lethargic bureaucratic creatures, and that, in order to make them useful to their intended purpose, it may be necessary to undo some of the results of the revolution of the 1970's not in order to return to the *status quo ante,* but simply in order to make sure certain things get done.

Now let us briefly look at each of the functional uses of intelligence, consider the degree to which a consensus on reform has emerged, and what the substantive controversies are about.

Analysis

In 1976, when a group of expert outsiders known as the B-Team, working from the same data base as the intelligence community, found serious fault with the community's estimates of Soviet strategic programs, many professional intelligence officers reacted defensively. They refused to admit that mistakes had been made. Some also tried to discredit members of the B-Team on grounds that it was improper for committed outsiders to judge the track record of intelligence analysts. Professionals reacted similarly when outside scholars confronted them with errors in their estimates of Soviet military spending, Soviet civil defense, the Iranian revolution, and the international oil market, among many topics. As embarrassment succeeded embarrassment, pressure mounted from Congress. In his last appearance before the Senate as DCI, George Bush attempted to defend the CIA's analytic record by questioning its critics' commitment to peace. Senator Hubert Humphrey replied that his own distinct political background did not keep him from appreciating facts and arguments on their merits, and that, *prima facie,* the critics' case looked good. Significantly, and despite some efforts on the staff level, policymakers have not generally supported intelligence community positions which were being seriously questioned in public discourse.

Thus, more and more professionals moved toward agreement with the following propositions: (1) the National Intelligence Estimates in particular, and the intelligence community's analytical products in general, had reflected errors that should not have been made; (2) the regular promotion of analysts responsible for a long series of bad estimates spreads disregard for quality within analytic organizations, and leads analysts to seek out the most advantageous cliques rather than the truth; (3) our analytic system does not call forth the analysts' best efforts. Analysts are seldom required to know the language of the area they study. Writing and rewriting to satisfy current requirements, and to provide ammunition for debates over policy, leaves them little time to learn their subject. The more senior they become, the more power they get to shape the product, the more their daily routine involves them in management and in policymaking, and keeps them away from substantive knowledge; (4) because National Intelligence Estimates are produced through a system of interagency consultations controlled by the CIA and staffed by managers who are expert primarily in word-smithing and bargaining, all too often their products consist of bland judgments which say less about the complexities of the subject than they do about the conflicting interests which went into the compromise; and (5) therefore, it may be necessary to bring into the analytical process more and more expert people who may have insights and points of views independent of those in the bureaucracy.

In January 1982, the CIA's Deputy Director for Intelligence (DDI) Robert Gates gave a speech to an assembly of CIA analysts which was immediately leaked to the *New York Times,* making many of these very points. Many professionals, recalling Director William Casey's approving reference to the concept of competitive analysis in his confirmation hearings, even began to speak favorably of this, the remedy advocated by many outsiders.

This does not mean that professional intelligence analysts have come to agree with outsiders' views of how their profession should be reformed. Indeed, many senior analysts, including DDI Gates, have countered that the current system of producing NIE's is competitive, because each of the agencies can vie (albeit with unequal bureaucratic means) to get its point of view into the document. They have succeeded in convincing the DCI that his and the President's commitment to competitive analysis would be fully satisfied by increasing the present system's competitiveness by bringing in more outside consultants, by showing the documents to a senior review panel earlier, and by offering them for judgment to the PFIAB more frequently. Special panels of consultants, chosen by the intelligence community, might also be brought in to look at specific problems. In addition, records would be kept of each analyst's production, so that the accuracy of his judgments might bear upon his promotions. Of course, those who coined the term ''competitive analysis'' meant by it something quite different, namely, that on the most important subjects different agencies should regularly produce their own distinct products, based on the same data, so that policymakers could read them side by side and compare their quality. Only thus, they argued, would each agency be spurred to doing its best, and be held accountable for the quality of its work by competitors whose interest would be to hold it accountable.

In 1981 the CIA's DDI undertook a physical reorganization much more vast than would have been required by competitive analysis, but quite unrelated to it. The Directorate's substantive divisions were dispersed in geographic divisions like those in the Directorate of Operations and the State Department. Thus, for example, the division of Soviet analysis now includes experts in economics, politics, weapons development. The division, however, is so large it cannot be physically accommodated at CIA headquarters. The new organization makes sense—but so did the old one. The functional scheme of organization did not appear to be at fault for any of the recent misestimates. The reorganization's effects remain to be seen.

In summary, the general feeling that something had to be done to improve intelligence analysis has led the CIA to introduce certain changes in that field. The relationship of those changes to quality is not readily apparent. Meanwhile, on November 24, 1982, the Defense Intelligence Agency established a Senior Executive Service for its analysts. Henceforth the DIA will have (as CIA has had for years) a means of attracting and keeping high-ranking analysts. The effect of this will not be felt in Washington for some time.

The real test of any analytical arrangement is its ability to make sense of the limited intelligence data we have, and to do so in time to provide policymakers, military planners, and commanders facts which they would not have known otherwise. Events inexorably establish track records.

Collection

Notwithstanding public and semi-public assertions by many professionals that our system of intelligence collection is about as it should be, a consensus seems to be developing—at least outside CIA—that major changes may be needed. In the course of Senate debates on the Intelligence Identities Protection Act, proponents quickly agreed with the opponents' contention that US clandestine agents abroad, nearly all of whom pose as employees of other US government agencies, were hardly covered at all. The fact that an overwhelming majority of the Congress went on to stipulate that anyone who tears off our clandestine officers' skimpy covers shall be punished does not mean that Congress thinks cover is adequate to the contrary. Some congressional specialists, and outsiders as well, have long argued that a human collection system based on "official cover" cannot achieve truly clandestine access to intelligence targets. This system's products tend to be comparable to diplomatic reports. Moreover, they argue, such a system suffers in times of diplomatic hostility, and cannot be expected to survive times of military hostility.

DCI William Casey seemed to agree with this when he appointed as head of the Directorate of Operations (DDO) an outsider, Max Hugel, thus suggesting that he intended to make greater use of the private sector in intelligence operations. That might have meant reducing the number of officially covered officers, putting more of them under non-official cover, and asking more Americans who are not employees of the CIA to undertake *ad hoc* intelligence assignments in the course of their normal work. Objection to this initiative by CIA professionals, far more than charges of questionable business dealings leveled against Mr. Hugel, accounted for the effort made in July 1981, after Mr. Hugel's resignation, to remove Mr. Casey. Although the effort failed, Mr. Casey appointed as DDO a career man basically dedicated to maintaining the present system, and did not again attempt to alter the clandestine service's *modus operandi*.

The chief argument for the present system is that it is relatively easy to administer, and produces a corps of career officers who know one another well. Officers under official cover also live with the

safety, immunities, and social position accorded to official representatives of the US government. Greater use of non-official cover would
mean that fewer officers would be in normal intra-office contact with
one another. Their *esprit de corps* might not be the same as it is now.
If a greater number of officers lived their daily lives among business
or professional people, or even as lower-ranking members of society,
instead of among senior officials of the US government, their ways
would be different. They would perhaps be less effective in interagency dealings than they are today. It would also be difficult to
administer a personnel system, leave, sick time, promotions, pen-
sions, and security, for people spending most of their lives out of
contact with their parent organization. Finally, a greater administrative infrastructure is required to support an officer under non-official
cover than is used now to support one under official cover.

These powerful objections notwithstanding, pressure for a change
in our human collection system is increasing. Military men bemoan
the lack of information available on hostile countries' military plans,
and doubt that such information is likely to be collected by human
collectors under official cover. Military men also are conscious of
the need for human collection in wartime. But they know that people
under official cover cannot operate as agents behind enemy lines,
nor will they have adequate motivation to recruit stay-behind net-
works. Therefore some military men, in addition to legislators and
some scholars, have begun to urge the broadening of human collection.

US technical collection has grown tremendously in importance
and in price. The U-2 photographic reconnaissance aircraft of the
late 1950's provided literally the first first-hand information available
on the quantity and state of development of Soviet strategic forces.
Overhead reconnaissance gave this country its first opportunity to
"visit" safely key points in the Soviet Union. The American technical intelligence system told us much of what we know about the
Soviet ballistic missiles.

The technology of intelligence improved radically at about the time
many in the US became interested in arms control. To this we owe
many of the features and the problems of our technical collection
system. First, we chose to follow the growth of technology in a
straightforward way. In most cases newer systems did precisely what
previous systems had done, only much much better and at much
higher cost. This led us to build fewer and fewer systems. Because

our technical programs were not serving any sort of strategic design, we never asked at what point a camera or a receiver were sensitive enough, and whether we ought to be building other kinds of things. Nor did we focus on the sort of technical collection system we would need to fight a war, and on its survivability. Secondly, the increasing sophistication, decreasing number, and non-survivability of technical systems fit well with the mission being energetically advocated by the Nixon, Ford, and Carter administrations—the monitoring of arms control treaties.

In recent years, however, skepticism about the effectiveness of arms control, the intimidating cost of further advances in technical systems, and the growing realization that this country needs intelligence to prepare to act in both political and military contingencies, have combined to force a reassessment of our course. Big, expensive *sui-generis* systems are still the order of the day, but few expect that day to last.

Counterintelligence

Counterintelligence (CI) consists of knowledge of the activities of hostile intelligence services, and action to frustrate those activities. Each of this country's intelligence agencies is involved in counterintelligence and contributes to it in some way. The FBI in its foreign counterintelligence program surveils suspected foreign intelligence officers and agents in the US and "runs" penetrations into hostile services within the US. CIA tries to recruit hostile intelligence officers abroad, and run whatever penetrations we may have there. The military services do try to identify and thwart attempts to penetrate or disrupt their units. The National Security Agency (NSA) provides material to all the agencies, while the Defense Intelligence Agency provides counterintelligence support to the Joint Chiefs of Staff. Each agency is responsible for its operational security. In the US, counterintelligence is the composite of all these activities.

There is no effective national system for assessing the threat which a hostile service or terrorist group poses to any one of our intelligence operations or systems, to any of our institutions, or to any policy— much less is there a coordinated system for doing anything about such threats. Although the maxim that no assessment is valid unless based on all available sources has long been recognized in the analysis of positive intelligence, the United States has not applied this insight to counterintelligence.

The most often cited reason for the fragmentation of counterintelligence is fear lest the combined forces of American intelligence be turned against Americans' civil liberties. In fact, however, the foreclosure by the National Security Act of 1947 of any law enforcement role for the CIA was never meant to inhibit full sharing of data and efforts by FBI and CIA in the field of counterintelligence.

Perhaps the primary reason for this fragmentation of American CI is a long tradition of professional jealousy between intelligence agencies. Although counterintelligence components cooperate with one another on selected cases, there has never been common analysis of a given field or problem. In other major countries, the services charged with CI operations at home may pool their information and form joint sections to work in given field as opposed to individual cases. Not so in the US.

Counterintelligence is at an inherent disadvantage in any country's intelligence system. One reason is that normal counterintelligence tasks often evoke resentment in other parts of the system. Counterintelligence analysts must take nothing for granted. They must question the information received from a source. If that information does not stand up under scrutiny, they must question the *bona fides* of the source himself. They must study the adequacy of any intelligence operation's security arrangements, searching for weaknesses, often working on the premise that the operation may have fallen under hostile control, or may have been under such control from its inception. Counterintelligence thus serves as a devil's advocate to offset the presumably more sanguine approach of the collector. A wide range of suspicions, targetted at all facets of an operation under scrutiny, are the stock-in-trade of professional counterintelligence. The immediate concerns of intelligence officers and of CI officers thus tend to be competitive with and at times antagonistic to those of intelligence collectors. No one likes to have his judgment questioned. On the other hand, there are obvious advantages in maintaining a healthy tension between collectors and counterintelligence officers. However, in the US, since 1975, such tension has been almost eliminated. In CIA, the Operations Directorate controls the careers of personnel in both counterintelligence and in clandestine collection via human sources. In the FBI, an agent is first and foremost a criminal investigator, even if he spends a major portion of his career in counterintelligence.

The two chief proposals for reform in counterintelligence are predicated on the belief that this failure to permit specialization in counterintelligence is a serious weakness. They call for the creation of career specialties for CI within each of the major intelligence agencies, and for the establishment of permanent mechanisms for interdisciplinary and interagency coordination of counterintelligence data and operations.

In February 1982, according to an article in the *Los Angeles Times* printed on 7 November, 1982, the President ordered the intelligence community to examine the need for these reforms and the ways in which they might be implemented. The intelligence community soon succeeded in reducing the scope (the bureaucratic term, "descoping") of the study to exclude "organizational questions." Thus, as they worked to produce the study ordered by the President, the several agencies were enabled to avoid addressing the adequacy of their "roles and missions," i.e., of their standing in relation to one another. Nevertheless, according to the *Los Angeles Times,* the completed study recognized the validity of the presidential directive's points, suggested minor palliatives, and left open the possibility of undertaking serious reforms. Knowledgeable officials warned, however, that bureaucratic resistance both to career counterintelligence specialization and, above all, to pooling of resources and data bases would be fierce.

Covert Action

Covertly influencing foreign events is now a relatively minor aspect of American intelligence operations. The need for effective means to exercise such influence became obvious to most Americans in the late 1970's when country after country, from Yemen to Nicaragua, fell under the control of forces supported by the Soviet Union. In fact, the CIA's ability to help friends and hinder enemies abroad, never as great as was supposed after back-to-back successes in Iran and Guatemala in 1953 and 1954, had nearly ceased to exist by 1980.

Shortages of money or the capacity to move it clandestinely, and of personnel able to carry out paramilitary tasks, though very serious, were never as debilitating as the near-total disappearance of strategic thinking, that is to say the disappearance from positions of power throughout the National Security decision-making apparatus of those willing and able to concoct reasonable, success-oriented plans for the United States. Even in 1980 there were covert actioneers who could plan and carry out basic operations such as press placements, or transfers of arms or money. But the ability to practice these techniques did not, and can never, spell the difference between victory and defeat in a given conflict. Most American covert action projects have long since failed to meet the "so what?" test. This is not primarily the CIA's fault. The near-demise of covert action is the result of a misunderstanding widespread in the US government.

Covert action is often viewed in the US as a measure of last resort, something to be done only when other political and economic options have failed, and when the only other option is to send in the Marines. Covert action is seen as a policy in itself, something undertaken in lieu of other policies, rather than one of numerous elements of policy (most of them overt) which can be used simultaneously in order to achieve success. Above all, and worst of all, covert action is seen as a way of pursuing a goal in foreign policy without having to explain to the American people why the goal is worth pursuing even at substantial cost. It is seen as a *politically* inexpensive form of commitment because, presumably, we can withdraw from covert failures without public embarrassment. In other words, covert actions, all too often, have been covert not to hide them from the enemy, but to spare policymakers the trouble of having to articulate their policies.

The decision to revitalize covert action did not have to wait for the Reagan Administration. Yet, under both presidents Carter and Reagan, increases in people and money devoted to covert action have not been matched by increased sophistication about how they are to be used. If the unnamed US officials who briefed the press on US policy in Nicaragua are correct, and the US funded opponents to the Sandinista regime just enough to harass that regime but without the intent or the intensity necessary to overthrow it, then current US covert action would be violating one of the most fundamental rules of human intercourse: Never do your enemy a little hurt; either get along with him or hurt him so badly as to make him incapable of hurting you.

Conclusion

The actual requirements for American intelligence in the 1980's are being set by an increasingly hostile world. Those in charge of our intelligence system must first recognize what our country will have to do in order to survive—if not to thrive—in the midst of such hostility. Only pursuant to such judgments will they be able wisely to plan intelligence collection, counterintelligence, analysis, and covert action. Judgments about what kind of world we live in and what we must do in it are not properly the province of the technicians of intelligence. They should emanate from the nation's elected officials and from senior appointed officials who live and work in the public eye. Only they are entitled to make such judgments, because only they can rightly translate the deliberate sense of the nation into commands which have both legal force and political support. To ask the technicians of intelligence to formulate a view of the world on the basis of which their own working lives would be restructured is to ask too much. Even as national leaders decide the consequences of the world situation for other operations of the government they head, they cannot shirk the responsibility of deciding what those consequences must be for intelligence. Professionals in this and other fields can offer valuable advice. But it is unrealistic for national leaders to expect the technicians of intelligence to offer wholly satisfactory proposals for redesigning the bureaucratic and professional system of which they are part. The lack of congruence between the world of the 1980's and the American intelligence system will continue to manifest itself in the form of surprises and defeats. The sooner our national leaders address that incongruence, the better will be the prospects for reshaping the US intelligence system to meet the needs of the day.

Consortium for the Study of Intelligence

Origin and Purpose

During the past decade, there has been a flood of material dealing with intelligence, particularly American intelligence and its relationship to national security and U.S. foreign policy. Some of this information has been made available in the writings of former intelligence officials. Other major sources include Congressional documents resulting from oversight activities, and documents released under the Freedom of Information Act.

As a result it has become increasingly possible to undertake objective, scholarly and unclassified research into the intelligence process and product, and to examine their relationship to U.S. decision making.

In light of these new circumstances, a group of social scientists from several academic institutions decided in April, 1979, to create a CONSORTIUM FOR THE STUDY OF INTELLIGENCE (CSI). Its membership includes political scientists, particularly specialists in international relations and U.S. foreign policy, historians, sociologists and professors of international and constitutional law.

CSI set for itself the following purposes:

 (i) To encourage teaching on both the graduate and undergraduate levels in the field of intelligence, as it relates to national security, foreign policy, law and ethics.

 (ii) To promote the development of a theory of intelligence—What is it, and what is its place in American national security policy? Comparative analysis with the practice and experience of other nations will be emphasized.

(iii) To encourage research into the intelligence process itself—analysis and estimates, clandestine collection, counterintelligence, and covert action; and to determine the feasibility of measuring efficiency or setting standards of efficiency so that the product can be improved.

(iv) To study the tensions between intelligence activities and the democratic and constitutional values of our society, and to seek the development of principles and methods for reconciling the two.

For various cultural and political reasons, the study of intelligence has too often been regarded by academicians as *ultra vires*. Their self-exclusion from the subject has inhibited an understanding of this significant instrument of the modern nation-state.

APPENDIX II

Executive Order 12333 "United States Intelligence Activities"

December 4, 1981

Executive Order 12333 of December 4, 1981

UNITED STATES INTELLIGENCE ACTIVITIES

[48 Fed. Reg. 59947 (1981)]

TABLE OF CONTENTS

Timely and accurate information about the activities, capabilities, plans, and intentions of foreign powers, organizations, and persons, and their agents, is essential to the national security of the United States. All reasonable and lawful means must be used to ensure that the United States will receive the best intelligence available. For that purpose, by virtue of the authority vested in me by the Constitution and statutes of the United States of America, including the National Security Act of 1947, as amended, and as President of the United States of America, in order to provide for the effective conduct of United States Intelligence activities and the protection of constitutional rights, it is hereby ordered as follows:

Part 1

Goals, Direction, Duties and Responsibilities With Respect to the National Intelligence Effort

1.1 *Goals.* The United States intelligence effort shall provide the President and the National Security Council with the necessary information on which to base decisions concerning the conduct and development of foreign defense and economic policy, and the protection of United States national interests from foreign security threats. All departments and agencies shall cooperate fully to fulfill this goal.

(a) Maximum emphasis should be given to fostering analytical competition among appropriate elements of the Intelligence Community.

(b) All means, consistent with applicable United States law and this Order, and with full consideration of the rights of United States persons, shall be used to develop intelligence information for the President and the National Security Council. A balanced approach between technical collection efforts and other means should be maintained and encouraged.

(c) Special emphasis should be given to detecting and countering espionage and other threats and activities directed by foreign intelligence services against the United States Government, or United States corporations, establishments, or persons.

(d) To the greatest extent possible consistent with applicable United States law and this Order, and with full consideration of the rights of United States persons, all agencies and departments should seek to ensure full and free exchange of information in order to derive maximum benifit from the United States intelligence effort.

1.2 *The National Security Council.*

(a) *Purpose.* The National Security Council (NSC) was established by the National Security Act of 1947 to advise the President with respect to the integration of domestic, foreign and military policies relating to the national security. The NSC shall act as the highest Executive Branch entity that provides review of, guidance for and direction to the conduct of all national foreign intelligence, counterintelligence, and special activities, and attendant policies and programs.

(b) *Committees.* The NSC shall establish such committees as may be necessary to carry out its functions and responsibilities under this Order. The NSC, or a committee established by it, shall consider and submit to the President a policy recommendation, including all dissents, on each special activity and shall review proposals for other sensitive intelligence operations.

1.3 *National Foreign Intelligence Advisory Groups.*

(a) *Establishment and Duties.* The Director of Central Intelligence shall establish such boards, councils, or groups as required for the purpose of obtaining advice from within the Intelligence Community concerning:

(1) Production, review and coordination of national foreign intelligence;

(2) Priorities for the National Foreign Intelligence Program budget;

(3) Interagency exchanges of foreign intelligence information;

(4) Arrangements with foreign governments on intelligence matters;

(5) Protection of intelligence sources and methods;

(6) Activities of common concern; and

(7) Such other matters as may be referred by the Director of Central Intelligence.

(b) *Membership.* Advisory groups established pursuant to this section shall be chaired by the Director of Central Intelligence or his designated representative and shall consist of senior representatives from organizations within the Intelligence Community and from departments or agencies containing such organizations, as designated by the Directive of Central Intelligence. Groups for consideration of substantive intelligence matters will include representatives of organizations involved in the collection, processing and analysis of intelligence. A senior representative of the Secretary of Commerce, the Attorney General, the Assistant to the President for National Security Affairs, and the Office of the Secretary of Defense shall be invited to participate in any group which deals with other than substantive intelligence matters.

1.4 *The Intelligence Community.* The agencies within the Intelligence Community shall, in accordance with applicable United States law and with the other provisions of this Order, conduct intelligence activities necessary for the conduct of foreign relations and the protection of the national security of the United States, including:

(a) Collection of information needed by the President, the National Security Council, the Secretaries of State and Defense, and other Executive Branch officials for the performance of their duties and responsibilities;

(b) Production and dissemination of intelligence;

(c) Collection of information concerning, and the conduct of activities to protect against, intelligence activities directed against the United States, international terrorist and international narcotics activities, and other hostile activities directed against the United States by foreign powers, organizations, persons, and their agents;

(d) Special activities;

(e) Administrative and support activities within the United States and abroad necessary for the performance of authorized activities; and

(f) Such other intelligence activities as the President may direct from time to time.

1.5 *Director of Central Intelligence.* In order to discharge the duties and responsibilities prescribed by law, the Director of Central Intelligence shall be responsible directly to the President and the NSC and shall:

(a) Act as the primary adviser to the President and the NSC on national foreign intelligence and provide the President and other officials in the Executive Branch with national foreign intelligence;

(b) Develop such objectives and guidance for the Intelligence Community as will enhance capabilities for responding to expected future needs for national foreign intelligence;

(c) Promote the development and maintenance of services of common concern by designated intelligence organizations on behalf of the Intelligence Community;

(d) Ensure implementation of special activities;

(e) Formulate policies concerning foreign intelligence and counterintelligence arrangements with foreign governments, coordinate foreign intelligence and counterintelligence relationships between agencies of the Intelligence Community and the intelligence or internal security services of foreign governments, and establish procedures governing the conduct of liaison by any department or agency with such services on narcotics activities;

(f) Participate in the development of procedures approved by the Attorney General governing criminal narcotics intelligence activities abroad to ensure that these activities are consistent with foreign intelligence programs;

(g) Ensure the establishment by the Intelligence Community of common security and access standards for managing and handling foreign intelligence systems, information, and products;

(h) Ensure that programs are developed which protect intelligence sources, methods, and analytical procedures;

(i) Establish uniform criteria for the determination of relative priorities for the transmission of critical national foreign intelligence, and advise the Secretary of Defense concerning the communications requirements of the Intelligence Community for the transmission of such intelligence;

(j) Establish appropriate staffs, committees, or other advisory groups to assist in the execution of the Director's responsibilities;

(k) Have full responsibility for production and dissemination of national foreign intelligence, and authority to levy analytic tasks on departmental intelligence production organizations, in consultation with those organizations, ensuring that appropriate mechanisms for competitive analysis are developed so that diverse points of view are considered fully and differences of judgment within the Intelligence Community are brought to the attention of national policymakers;

(l) Ensure the timely exploitation and dissemination of data gathered by national foreign intelligence collection means, and ensure that the resulting intelligence is disseminated immediately to appropriate government entities and military commands;

(m) Establish mechanisms which translate national foreign intelligence objectives and priorities approved by the NSC into specific guidance for the Intelligence Community, resolve conflicts in tasking priority, provide to departments and agencies having information collection capabilities that are not part of the National Foreign Intelligence Program advisory tasking concerning collection of national foreign intelligence, and provide for the development of plans and arrangements for transfer of required collection tasking authority to the Secretary of Defense when directed by the President;

(n) Develop, with the advice of the program managers and departments and agencies concerned, the consolidated National Foreign Intelligence Program budget, and present it to the President and the Congress;

(o) Review and approve all requests for reprogramming National Foreign Intelligence Program funds, in accordance with guidelines established by the Office of Management and Budget;

(p) Monitor National Foreign Intelligence Program implementation, and, as necessary, conduct program and performance audits and evaluations;

(q) Together with the Secretary of Defense, ensure that there is no unnecessary overlap between national foreign intelligence programs and Department of Defense intelligence programs consistent with the requirement to develop competitive analysis, and provide to and obtain from the Secretary of Defense all information necessary for this purpose;

(r) In accordance with law and relevant procedures approved by the Attorney General under this Order, give the heads of the departments and agencies access to all intelligence, developed by the CIA or the staff elements of the Director of Central Intelligence, relevant to the national intelligence needs of the departments and agencies; and

(s) Facilitate the use of national intelligence products by Congress in a secure manner.

1.6 *Duties and Responsibilities of the Heads of Executive Branch Departments and Agencies.*

(a) The heads of all Executive Branch departments and agencies shall, in accordance with law and relevant procedures approved by the

Attorney General under this Order, give the Director of Central Intelligence access to all information relevant to the national intelligence needs of the United States, and shall give due consideration to the requests from the Director of Central Intelligence for appropriate support for Intelligence Community activities.

(b) The heads of departments and agencies involved in the National Foreign Intelligence Program shall ensure timely development and submission to the Director of Central Intelligence by the program managers and heads of component activities of proposed national programs and budgets in the format designated by the Director of Central Intelligence, and shall also ensure that the Director of Central Intelligence is provided, in a timely and responsive manner, all information necessary to perform the Director's program and budget responsibilities.

(c) The heads of departments and agencies involved in the National Foreign Intelligence Program may appeal to the President decisions by the Director of Central Intelligence on budget or reprogramming matters of the National Foreign Intelligence Program.

1.7 *Senior Officials of the Intelligence Community.* The heads of departments and agencies with organizations in the Intelligence Community or the heads of such organizations, as appropriate, shall:

(a) Report to the Attorney General possible violations of federal criminal laws by employees and of specified federal criminal laws by any other persons as provided in procedures agreed upon by the Attorney General and the head of the department or agency concerned, in a matter consistent with the protection of intelligence sources and methods, as specified in those procedures;

(b) In any case involving serious or continuing breaches of security, recommendations to the Attorney General that the case be referred to the FBI for further investigation;

(c) Furnish the Director of Central Intelligence and the NSC, in accordance with applicable law and procedures approved by the Attorney General under this Order, the information required for the performance of their respective duties;

(d) Report to the Intelligence Oversight Board, and keep the Director of Central Intelligence appropriately informed, concerning any intelligence activities of their organizations that they have reason to believe may be unlawful or contrary to Executive order or Presidential directive;

(e) Protect intelligence and intelligence sources and methods from unauthorized disclosure consistent with guidance from the Director of Central Intelligence;

(f) Disseminate intelligence to cooperating foreign governments under arrangements established or agreed to by the Director of Central Intelligence;

(g) Participate in the development of procedures approved by the Attorney General governing production and dissemination of intelligence resulting from criminal narcotics intelligence activities abroad if their departments, agencies, or organizations have intelligence responsibilities for foreign or domestic narcotics production and trafficking;

(h) Instruct their employees to cooperate fully with the Intelligence Oversight Board; and

(i) Ensure that the Inspectors General and General Counsels for their organizations have access to any information necessary to perform their duties assigned by this order.

1.8 *The Central Intelligence Agency.* All duties and responsibilities of the CIA shall be related to the intelligence functions set out below. As authorized by this Order; the National Security Act of 1947, as amended; the CIA Act of 1949, as amended; appropriate directives or other applicable law, the CIA shall:

(a) Collect, produce and disseminate foreign intelligence and counterintelligence, including information not otherwise obtainable. The collection of foreign intelligence or counterintelligence within the United States shall be coordinated with FBI as required by procedures agreed upon by the Director of Central Intelligence and the Attorney General;

(b) Collect, produce and disseminate intelligence on foreign aspects of narcotics production and trafficking;

(c) Conduct counterintelligence activities outside the United States and, without assuming or performing any internal security functions, conduct counterintelligence activities within the United States in coordination with the FBI as required by procedures agreed upon the Director of Central Intelligence and the Attorney General;

(d) Coordinate counterintelligence activities and the collection of information not otherwise obtainable when conducted outside the United States by other departments and agencies;

(e) Conduct special activities approved by the President. No agency except the CIA (or the Armed Forces of the United States in time of war declared by Congress or during any period covered by a report from the President to the Congress under the War Powers Resolution (87 Stat. 885)) may conduct any special activity unless the President determines that another agency is more likely to achieve a particular objective;

(f) Conduct services of common concern for the Intelligence Community as directed by the NSC;

(g) Carry out or contract for research, development and procurement of technical systems and devices relating to authorized functions;

(h) Protect the security of its installations, activities, information, property, and employees by appropriate means, including such investigations of applicants, employees, contractors, and other persons with similar associations with the CIA as are necessary; and

(i) Conduct such administrative and technical support activities within and outside the United States as are necessary to perform the functions described in sections (a) and through (h) above, including procurement and essential cover and proprietary arrangements.

1.9 *The Department of State.* The Secretary of State shall:

(a) Overtly collect information relevant to United States foreign policy concerns;

(b) Produce and disseminate foreign intelligence relating to United States foreign policy as required for the execution of the Secretary's responsibilities;

(c) Disseminate, as appropriate, reports received from United States diplomatic and consular posts;

(d) Transmit reporting requirements of the Intelligence Community to the Chiefs of United States Missions abroad; and

(e) Support Chiefs of Missions in discharging their statutory responsibilities for direction and coordination of mission activities.

1.10 *The Department of the Treasury.* The Secretary of the Treasury shall:

(a) Overtly collect foreign financial and monetary information;

(b) Participate with the Department of State in the overt collection of general foreign economic information;

(c) Produce and disseminate foreign intelligence relating to United States economic policy as required for the execution of the Secretary's responsibilities; and

(d) Conduct, through the United States Secret Service, activities to determine the existence and capability of surveillance equipment being used against the President of the United States, the Executive Office of the President, and, as authorized by the Secretary of the Treasury or the President, other Secret Service protectees and United States officials. No information shall be acquired intentionally through such activities except to protect against such surveillance, and those activities shall be conducted pursuant to procedures agreed upon by the Secretary of the Treasury and the Attorney General.

1.11 *The Department of Defense.* The Secretary of Defense shall:

(a) Collect national foreign intelligence and be responsive to collection tasking by the Director of Central Intelligence;

(b) Collect, produce and disseminate military and military-related foreign intelligence and counterintelligence as required for execution of the Secretary's responsibilities;

(c) Conduct programs and missions necessary to fulfill national, departmental and tactical foreign intelligence requirements;

(d) Conduct counterintelligence activities in support of Department of Defense components outside the United States in coordination with the CIA, and within the United States in coordination with the FBI pursuant to procedures agreed upon by the Secretary of Defense and the Attorney General;

(e) Conduct, as the executive agent of the United States Government, signals intelligence and communications security activities, except as otherwise directed by the NSC;

(f) Provide for the timely transmission of critical intelligence, as defined by the Director of Central Intelligence, within the United States Government;

(g) Carry out or contract for research, development and procurement of technical systems and devices relating to authorized intelligence functions;

(h) Protect the security of Department of Defense installations, activities, property, information, and employees by appropriate means, including such investigations of applicants, employees, contractors, and other persons with similar associations with the Department of Defense as are necessary;

(i) Establish and maintain military intelligence relationships and military intelligence exchange programs with selected cooperative foreign defense establishments and international organizations, and ensure that such relationships and programs are in accordance with policies formulated by the Director of Central Intelligence;

(j) Direct, operate, control and provide fiscal management for the National Security Agency and for defense and military intelligence and national reconnaissance entities; and

(k) Conduct such administrative and technical support activities within and outside the United States as are necessary to perform the functions described in sections (a) through (j) above.

1.12 *Intelligence Components Utilized by the Secretary of Defense.* In carrying out the responsibilities assigned in section 1.11, the Secretary of Defense is authorized to utilize the following:

(a) *Defense Intelligence Agency,* whose responsibilities shall include;

(1) Collection, production, or, through tasking and coordination, provision of military and military-related intelligence for the Secretary of Defense, the Joint Chiefs of Staff, other Defense components, and, as appropriate, non-Defense agencies;

(2) Collection and provision of military intelligence for national foreign intelligence and counterintelligence products;

(3) Coordination of all Department of Defense intelligence collection requirements;

(4) Management of the Defense Attache system; and

(5) Provision of foreign intelligence and counterintelligence staff support as directed by the Joint Chiefs of Staff.

(b) *National Security Agency,* whose responsibilities shall include:

(1) Establishment and operation of an effective unified organization for signals intelligence activities, except for the delegation of operational control over certain operations that are conducted through other elements of the Intelligence Community. No other department or agency may engage in signals intelligence activities except pursuant to a delegation by the Secretary of Defense;

(2) Control of signals intelligence collection and processing activities, including assignment of resources to an appropriate agent for such periods and tasks as required for the direct support of military commanders;

(3) Collection of signals intelligence information for national foreign intelligence purposes in accordance with guidance from the Director of Central Intelligence;

(4) Processing of signals intelligence data for national foreign intelligence purposes in accordance with guidance from the Director of Central Intelligence;

(5) Dissemination of signals intelligence information for national foreign intelligence purposes to authorized elements of the Government, including the military services, in accordance with guidance from the Director of Central Intelligence;

(6) Collection, processing and dissemination of signals intelligence information for counterintelligence purposes;

(7) Provision of signals intelligence support for the conduct of military operations in accordance with tasking, priorities, and standards of timeliness assigned by the Secretary of Defense. If provision of such support requires use of national collection systems, these systems will be tasked within existing guidance from the Director of Central Intelligence;

(8) Executing the responsibilities of the Secretary of Defense as executive agent for the communications security of the United States Government;

(9) Conduct of research and development to meet the needs of the United States for signals intelligence and communications security;

(10) Protection of the security of its installations, activities, property, information, and employees by appropriate means, including such investigations of applicants, employees, contractors, and other persons with similar associations with the NSA as are necessary;

(11) Prescribing, within its field of authorized operations, security regulations covering operating practices, including the transmission, handling and distribution of signals intelligence and communications security material within and among the elements under control of the Director of the NSA, and exercising the necessary supervisory control to ensure compliance with the regulations;

(12) Conduct of foreign cryptologic liaison relationships, with liaison for intelligence purposes conducted in accordance with policies formulated by the Director of Central Intelligence; and

(13) Conduct of such administrative and technical support activities within and outside the United States as are necessary to perform the functions described in sections (1) through (12) above, including procurement.

(c) *Offices for the collection of specialized intelligence through reconnaissance programs,* whose responsibilities shall include:

(1) Carrying out consolidated reconnaissance programs for specialized intelligence;

(2) Responding to tasking in accordance with procedures established by the Director of Central Intelligence; and

(3) Delegating authority to the various departments and agencies for research, development, procurement, and operation of designated means of collection.

(d) *The foreign intelligence and counterintelligence elements of the Army, Navy, Air Force, and Marine Corps,* whose responsibilities shall include:

(1) Collection, production and dissemination of military and military-related foreign intelligence and counterintelligence, and information on the foreign aspects of narcotics production and trafficking. When collection is conducted in response to national foreign intelligence requirements, it will be conducted in accordance with guidance from the Director of Central Intelligence. Collection of national foreign intelligence, not otherwise obtainable, outside the United States shall be coordinated with the CIA, and such collection within the United States shall be coordinated with the FBI;

(2) Conduct of counterintelligence activities outside the United States in coordination with the CIA, and within the United States in coordination with the FBI; and

(3) Monitoring of the development, procurement and management of tactical intelligence systems and equipment and conducting related research, development, and test and evaluation activities.

(e) Other offices within the Department of Defense appropriate for conduct of the intelligence missions and responsibilities assigned to the Secretary of Defense. If such other offices are used for intelligence purposes, the provisions of Part 2 of this Order shall apply to those offices when used for those purposes.

1.13 *The Department of Energy.* The Secretary of Energy shall:

(a) Participate with the Department of State in overtly collecting information with respect to foreign energy matters;

(b) Produce and disseminate foreign intelligence necessary for the Secretary's responsibilities;

(c) Participate in formulating intelligence collection and analysis requirements where the special expert capability of the Department can contribute; and

(d) Provide expert technical, analytical and research capability to other agencies within the Intelligence Community.

1.14 *The Federal Bureau of Investigation.* Under the supervision of the Attorney General and pursuant to such regulations as the Attorney General may establish, the Director of the FBI shall:

(a) Within the United States conduct counterintelligence and coordinate counterintelligence activities of other agencies within the Intelligence Community. When a counterintelligence activity of the FBI involves military or civilian personnel of the Department of Defense, the FBI shall coordinate with the Department of Defense;

(b) Conduct counterintelligence activities outside the United States in coordination with the CIA as required by procedures agreed upon by the Director of Central Intelligence and the Attorney General;

(c) Conduct within the United States, when requested by officials of the Intelligence Community designated by the President, activities undertaken to collect foreign intelligence or support foreign intelligence collection requirements of other agencies within the Intelligence Community, or, when requested by the Director of the National Security Agency, to support the communications security activities of the United States Government;

(d) Produce and disseminate foreign intelligence and counterintelligence; and

(e) Carry out or contract for research, development and procurement of technical systems and devices relating to the functions authorized above.

Part 2

Conduct of Intelligence Activities

2.1 *Need.* Accurate and timely information about the capabilities, intentions and activities of foreign powers, organizations, or persons and their agents is essential to informed decisionmaking in the areas of national defense and foreign relations. Collection of such information is a priority objective and will be pursued in a vigorous, innovative and responsible manner that is consistent with the Constitution and applicable law and respectful of the principles upon which the United States was founded.

2.2 *Purpose.* This Order is intended to enhance human and technical collection techniques, especially those undertaken abroad, and the acquisition of significant foreign intelligence, as well as the detection and countering of international terrorist activities and espionage conducted by foreign powers. Set forth below are certain general principles that, in addition to and consistent with applicable laws, are intended to achieve the proper balance between the acquisition of essential information and protection of individual interests. Nothing in this Order shall be construed to apply to or interfere with any authorized civil or criminal law enforcement responsibility of any department or agency.

2.3 *Collection of Information.* Agencies within the Intelligence Community are authorized to collect, retain or disseminate information concerning United States persons only in accordance with procedures established by the head of the agency concerned and approved by the Attorney General, consistent with the authorities provided by Part 1 of this Order. Those procedures shall permit collection, retention and dissemination of the following types of information:

(a) Information that is publicly available or collected with the consent of the person concerned;

(b) Information constituting foreign intelligence or counter-intelligence, including such information concerning corporations or other commercial organizations. Collection within the United States of foreign intelligence not otherwise obtainable shall be undertaken by the FBI or, when significant foreign intelligence is sought, by other authorized agencies of the Intelligence Community, provided that no foreign intelligence collection by such agencies may be undertaken for the purpose of acquiring information concerning the domestic activities of United States persons;

(c) Information obtained in the course of a lawful foreign intelligence, counterintelligence, international narcotics or international terrorism investigation;

(d) Information needed to protect the safety of any persons or organizations, including those who are targets, victims or hostages of international terrorist organizations;

(e) Information needed to protect foreign intelligence or counterintelligence sources or methods from unauthorized disclosure. Collection within the United States shall be undertaken by the FBI except that other agencies of the Intelligence Community may also collect such information concerning present or former employees, present or former intelligence agency contractors or their present or former employees, or applicants for any such employment or contracting;

(f) Information concerning persons who are reasonably believed to be potential sources or contacts for the purpose of determining their suitability or credibility;

(g) Information arising out of a lawful personnel, physical or communications security investigation;

(h) Information acquired by overhead reconnaissance not directed at specific United States persons;

(i) Incidentally obtained information that may indicate involvement in activities that may violate federal, state, local or foreign laws; and

(j) Information necessary for administrative purposes.
In addition, agencies within the Intelligence Community may disseminate information, other than information derived from signals intelligence, to each appropriate agency within the Intelligence Community for purposes of allowing the recipient agency to determine whether the information is relevant to its responsibilities and can be retained by it.

2.4 *Collection Techniques.* Agencies within the Intelligence Community shall use the least intrusive collection techniques feasible within the United States or directed against United States persons abroad. Agencies are not authorized to use such techniques as electronic surveillance, unconsented physical search, mail surveillance, physical surveillance, or monitoring devices unless they are in accordance with procedures established by the head of the agency concerned and approved by the Attorney General. Such procedures shall protect constitutional and other legal rights and limit use of such information to lawful governmental purposes. These procedures shall not authorize:

(a) The CIA to engage in electronic surveillance within the United States except for the purpose of training, testing, or conducting countermeasures to hostile electronic surveillance;

(b) Unconsented physical searches in the United States by agencies other than the FBI, except for:

(1) Searches by counterintelligence elements of the military services directd against military personnel within the United States or abroad for intelligence purposes, when authorized by a military commander empowered to approve physical searches for law inforcement purposes, based upon a finding of probable cause to believe that such persons are acting as agents of foreign powers; and

(2) Searches by CIA of personal property of non-United States persons lawfully in its possession.

(c) Physical surveillance of a United States person in the United States by agencies other than the FBI, except for:

(1) Physical surveillance of present or former employees, present or former intelligence agency contractors or their present of former employees, or applicants for any such employment or contracting; and

(2) Physical surveillance of a military person employed by a nonintelligence element of a military service.

(d) Physical surveillance of a United States person abroad to collect foreign intelligence, except to obtain significant information that cannot reasonably be acquired by other means.

2.5 *Attorney General Approval.* The Attorney General hereby is delegated the power to approve the use for intelligence purposes, within the United States or against a United States person abroad, of any technique for which a warrant would be required if undertaken for law enforcement purposes, provided that such techniques shall not be undertaken unless the Attorney General has determined in each case that there is probable cause to believe that the technique is directed against a foreign power or an agent of a foreign power. Electronic surveillance, as defined in the Foreign Intelligence Surveillance Act of 1978, shall be conducted in accordance with that Act, as well as this Order.

2.6 *Assistance to Law Enforcement Authorities.* Agencies within the Intelligence Community are authorized to:

(a) Cooperate with appropriate law enforcement agencies for the purpose of protecting the employees, information, property and facilities of any agency within the Intelligence Community;

(b) Unless otherwise precluded by law or this Order, participate in law enforcement activities to investigate or prevent clandestine intelligence activities by foreign powers, or international terrorist or narcotics activities;

(c) Provide specialized equipment, technical knowledge, or assistance of expert personnel for use by any department or agency, or, when lives are endangered, to support local law enforcement agencies. Provision of assistance by expert personnel shall be approved in each case by the General Counsel of the providing agency; and

(d) Render any other assistance and cooperation to law enforcement authorities not precluded by applicable law.

2.7 *Contracting.* Agencies within the Intelligence Community are authorized to enter into contracts or arrangements for the provision of goods or services with private companies or institutions in the United States and need not reveal the sponsorship of such contracts or arrangements for authorized intelligence purposes. Contracts or arrangements with academic institutions may be undertaken only with the consent of appropriate officials of the institution.

2.8 *Consistency With Other Laws.* Nothing in this Order shall be construed to authorize any activity in violation of the Constitution or statutes of the United States.

2.9 *Undisclosed Participation in Organizations Within the United States.* No one acting on behalf of agencies within the Intelligence Community may join or otherwise participate in any organization in the United States on behalf of any agency within the Intelligence Community without disclosing his intelligence affiliation to appropriate officials of the organization, except in accordance with procedures established by the head of the agency concerned and approved by the Attorney General. Such participation shall be authorized only if it is essential to achieving lawful purposes as determined by the agency head or designee. No such participation may be undertaken for the purpose of influencing the activity of the organization or its members except in cases where:

(a) The participation is undertaken on behalf of the FBI in the course of a lawful investigation; or

(b) The organization concerned is composed primarily of individuals who are not United States persons and is reasonably believed to be acting on behalf of a foreign power.

2.10 *Human Experimentation.* No agency within the Intelligence Community shall sponsor, contract for or conduct research on human subjects except in accordance with guidelines issued by the Department of Health and Human Services. The subject's informed consent shall be documented as required by those guidelines.

2.11 *Prohibition on Assassination.* No person employed by or acting on behalf of the United States Government shall engage in, or conspire to engage in, assassination.

2.12 *Indirect Participation.* No agency of the Intelligence Community shall participate in or request any person to undertake activities forbidden by this Order.

Part 3

General Provisions

3.1 *Congressional Oversight.* The duties and responsibilities of the Director of Central Intelligence and the heads of other departments, agencies, and entities engaged in intelligence activities to cooperate with the Congress in the conduct of its responsibilities for oversight of intelligence activities shall be as provided in title 50, United States Code, section 413. The requirements of section 662 of the Foreign Assistance Act of 1961, as amended (22 U.S.C. 2422), and section 501 of the National Security Act of 1947, as amended (50 U.S.C. 413), shall apply to all special activities as defined in this Order.

3.2 *Implementation.* The NSC, the Secretary of Defense, the Attorney General, and the Director of Central Intelligence shall issue such appropriate directives and procedures as are necessary to implement this Order. Heads of agencies within the Intelligence Community shall issue appropriate supplementary directives and procedures consistent with this Order. The Attorney General shall provide a statement of reasons for not approving any procedures established by the head of an agency in the Intelligence Community other than the FBI. The National Security Council may establish procedures in instances where the agency head and the Attorney General are unable to reach agreement on other than constitutional or other legal grounds.

3.3 *Procedures.* Until the procedures required by this Order have been established, the activities herein authorized which require procedures shall be conducted in accordance with existing procedures or requirements established under Executive Order No. 12036. Procedures required by this Order shall be established as expeditiously as possible. All procedures promulgated pursuant to this Order shall be made available to the congressional intelligence committees.

3.4 *Definitions.* For the purposes of this Order, the following terms shall have these meanings:

(a) *Counterintelligence* means information gathered and activities conducted to protect against espionage, other intelligence activities, sabotage, or assassinations conducted for or on behalf of foreign powers, organizations or persons, or international terrorist activities, but not including personnel, physical, document or communications security programs.

(b) *Electronic surveillance* means acquisition of a nonpublic communication by electronic means without the consent of a person who is a party to an electronic communication or, in the case of a nonelectronic communication, without the consent of a person who is visably present at the place of communication, but not including the use of radio direction-finding equipment solely to determine the location of a transmitter.

(c) *Employee* means a person employed by, assigned to or acting for an agency within the Intelligence Community.

(d) *Foreign intelligence* means information relating to the capabilities, intentions and activities of foreign powers, organizations or persons, but not including counterintelligence except for information on international terrorist activities.

(e) *Intelligence activities* means all activities that agencies within the Intelligence Community are authorized to conduct pursuant to this Order.

(f) *Intelligence Community* and *agencies within the Intelligence Community* refer to the following agencies or organizations:

(1) The Central Intelligence Agency (CIA);

(2) The National Security Agency (NSA);

(3) The Defense Intelligence Agency (DIA);

(4) The offices within the Department of Defense for the collection of specialized national foreign intelligence through reconnaissance programs;

(5) The Bureau of Intelligence and Research of the Department of State;

(6) The intelligence elements of the Army, Navy, Air Force, and Marine Corps, the Federal Bureau of Investigation (FBI), the Department of the Treasury, and the Department of Energy; and

(7) The staff elements of the Director of Central Intelligence.

(g) *The National Foreign Intelligence Program* includes the programs listed below, but its composition shall be subject to review by the National Security Council and modification by the President:

(1) The programs of the CIA;

(2) The Consolidated Cryptologic Program, the General Defense Intelligence Program, and the programs of the offices within the Department of Defense for the collection of specialized national foreign intelligence through reconnaissance, except such elements as the Director of Central Intelligence and the Secretary of Defense agree should be excluded;

(3) Other programs of agencies within the Intelligence Community designated jointly by the Director of Central Intelligence and the head of the department or by the President as national foreign intelligence or counterintelligence activities;

(4) Activities of the staff elements of the Director of Central Intelligence;

(5) Activities to acquire the intelligence required for the planning and conduct of tactical operations by the United States military forces are not included in the National Foreign Intelligence Program.

(h) *Special activities* means activities conducted in support of national foreign policy objectives abroad which are planned and executed so that the role of the United States Government is not apparent or acknowledged publicly, and functions in support of such activities, but which are not intended to influence United States political processes, public opinion, policies, or media and do not include diplomatic activities or the collection and production of intelligence or related support functions.

(i) *United States person* means a United States citizen, an alien known by the intelligence agency concerned to be a permanent resident alien, an unincorporated association substantially composed of United States citizens or permanent resident aliens, or a corporation incorporated in the United States, except for a corporation directed and controlled by a foreign government or governments.

3.5 *Purpose and Effect.* This Order is intended to control and provide direction and guidance to the Intelligence Community. Nothing contained herein or in any procedures promulgated hereunder is intended to confer any substantive or procedural right or privilege on any person or organization.

3.6 *Revocation.* Executive Order No. 12036 of Janury 24, 1978, as amended, entitled "United States Intelligence Activities," is revoked.

Ronald Reagan

THE WHITE HOUSE,
December 4, 1981.

APPENDIX III

Intelligence Identities Protection Act, 1982

June 23, 1982

PUBLIC LAW 97-200—JUNE 23, 1982

Public Law 97-200
97th Congress

An Act

June 23, 1982
[H.R. 4]

To amend the National Security Act of 1947 to prohibit the unauthorized disclosure of information identifying certain United States intelligence officers, agents, informants, and sources.

Be it enacted by the Senate and House of Representatives of the United States of America in Congress assembled, That this Act may be cited as the "Intelligence Identities Protection Act of 1982".

Intelligence Identities Protection Act of 1982.
50 USC 401 note.

SEC. 2. (a) The National Security Act of 1947 is amended by adding at the end thereof the following new title:

"TITLE VI—PROTECTION OF CERTAIN NATIONAL SECURITY
INFORMATION

"PROTECTION OF IDENTITIES OF CERTAIN UNITED STATES UNDERCOVER
INTELLIGENCE OFFICERS, AGENTS, INFORMANTS, AND SOURCES

50 USC 421.

"SEC. 601. (a) Whoever, having or having had authorized access to classified information that identifies a covert agent, intentionally discloses any information identifying such covert agent to any individual not authorized to receive classified information, knowing that the information disclosed so identifies such covert agent and that the United States is taking affirmative measures to conceal such covert agent's intelligence relationship to the United States, shall be fined not more than $50,000 or imprisoned not more than ten years, or both.

"(b) Whoever, as a result of having authorized access to classified information, learns the identity of a covert agent and intentionally discloses any information identifying such covert agent to any individual not authorized to receive classified information, knowing that the information disclosed so identifies such covert agent and that the United States is taking affirmative measures to conceal such covert agent's intelligence relationship to the United States, shall be fined not more than $25,000 or imprisoned not more than five years, or both.

"(c) Whoever, in the course of a pattern of activities intended to identify and expose covert agents and with reason to believe that such activities would impair or impede the foreign intelligence activities of the United States, discloses any information that identifies an individual as a covert agent to any individual not authorized to receive classified information, knowing that the information disclosed so identifies such individual and that the United States is taking affirmative measures to conceal such individual's classified intelligence relationship to the United States, shall be fined not more than $15,000 or imprisoned not more than three years, or both.

"DEFENSES AND EXCEPTIONS

50 USC 422.

"SEC. 602. (a) It is a defense to a prosecution under section 601 that before the commission of the offense with which the defendant is charged, the United States had publicly acknowledged or revealed the intelligence relationship to the United States of the individual the disclosure of whose intelligence relationship to the United States is the basis for the prosecution.

"(b)(1) Subject to paragraph (2), no person other than a person committing an offense under section 601 shall be subject to prosecution under such section by virtue of section 2 or 4 of title 18, United States Code, or shall be subject to prosecution for conspiracy to commit an offense under such section.

"(2) Paragraph (1) shall not apply (A) in the case of a person who acted in the course of a pattern of activities intended to identify and expose covert agents and with reason to believe that such activities would impair or impede the foreign intelligence activities of the United States, or (B) in the case of a person who has authorized access to classified information.

"(c) It shall not be an offense under section 601 to transmit information described in such section directly to the Select Committee on Intelligence of the Senate or to the Permanent Select Committee on Intelligence of the House of Representatives.

Information, transmittal to congressional committees.

"(d) It shall not be an offense under section 601 for an individual to disclose information that solely identifies himself as a covert agent.

"REPORT

"SEC. 603. (a) The President, after receiving information from the Director of Central Intelligence, shall submit to the Select Committee on Intelligence of the Senate and the Permanent Select Committee on Intelligence of the House of Representatives an annual report on measures to protect the identities of covert agents, and on any other matter relevant to the protection of the identities of covert agents.

50 USC 423.

"(b) The report described in subsection (a) shall be exempt from any requirement for publication or disclosure. The first such report shall be submitted no later than February 1, 1983.

"EXTRATERRITORIAL JURISDICTION

"SEC. 604. There is jurisdiction over an offense under section 601 committed outside the United States if the individual committing the offense is a citizen of the United States or an alien lawfully admitted to the United States for permanent residence (as defined in section 101(a)(20) of the Immigration and Nationality Act).

50 USC 424.

8 USC 1101.

"PROVIDING INFORMATION TO CONGRESS

"SEC. 605. Nothing in this title may be construed as authority to withhold information from the Congress or from a committee of either House of Congress.

50 USC 425.

"DEFINITIONS

"SEC. 606. For the purposes of this title:

50 USC 426.

"(1) The term 'classified information' means information or material designated and clearly marked or clearly represented, pursuant to the provisions of a statute or Executive order (or a regulation or order issued pursuant to a statute or Executive order), as requiring a specific degree of protection against unauthorized disclosure for reasons of national security.

"(2) The term 'authorized', when used with respect to access to classified information, means having authority, right, or permission pursuant to the provisions of a statute, Executive order, directive of the head of any department or agency engaged in foreign intelligence or counterintelligence activities, order of any United States court, or provisions of any Rule of the House of Representatives or resolution of the Senate which assigns responsibility within the respective House of Congress for the oversight of intelligence activities.

"(3) The term 'disclose' means to communicate, provide, impart, transmit, transfer, convey, publish, or otherwise make available.

"(4) The term 'covert agent' means—

"(A) an officer or employee of an intelligence agency or a member of the Armed Forces assigned to duty with an intelligence agency—

"(i) whose identity as such an officer, employee, or member is classified information, and

"(ii) who is serving outside the United States or has within the last five years served outside the United States; or

"(B) a United States citizen whose intelligence relationship to the United States is classified information, and—

"(i) who resides and acts outside the United States as an agent of, or informant or source of operational assistance to, an intelligence agency, or

"(ii) who is at the time of the disclosure acting as an agent of, or informant to, the foreign counterintelligence or foreign counterterrorism components of the Federal Bureau of Investigation; or

"(C) an individual, other than a United States citizen, whose past or present intelligence relationship to the United States is classified information and who is a present or former agent of, or a present or former informant or source of operational assistance to, an intelligence agency.

"(5) The term 'intelligence agency' means the Central Intelligence Agency, a foreign intelligence component of the Department of Defense, or the foreign counterintelligence or foreign counterterrorism components of the Federal Bureau of Investigation.

"(6) The term 'informant' means any individual who furnishes information to an intelligence agency in the course of a confidential relationship protecting the identity of such individual from public disclosure.

"(7) The terms 'officer' and 'employee' have the meanings given such terms by section 2104 and 2105, respectively, of title 5, United States Code.

"(8) The term 'Armed Forces' means the Army, Navy, Air Force, Marine Corps, and Coast Guard.

"(9) The term 'United States', when used in a geographic sense, means all areas under the territorial sovereignty of the United States and the Trust Territory of the Pacific Islands.

"(10) The term 'pattern of activities' requires a series of acts with a common purpose or objective.".

PUBLIC LAW 97-200—JUNE 23, 1982 96 STAT. 125

(b) The table of contents at the beginning of such Act is amended by adding at the end thereof the following:

"TITLE VI—PROTECTION OF CERTAIN NATIONAL SECURITY INFORMATION

"Sec. 601. Protection of identities of certain United States undercover intelligence officers, agents, informants, and sources.
"Sec. 602. Defenses and exceptions.
"Sec. 603. Report.
"Sec. 604. Extraterritorial jurisdiction.
"Sec. 605. Providing information to Congress.
"Sec. 606. Definitions.".

Approved June 23, 1982.

APPENDIX IV

Intelligence Authorization Act Fiscal Year 1981

[Extracts.]

[Amendment to the Hughes-Ryan Amendment]

PUBLIC LAW 96-450
OCT. 14, 1980
[Extracts]

TITLE IV-GENERAL PROVISIONS

SEC. 407. (a) Section 662 of the Foreign Assistance Act of 1961 (22 U.S.C. 2422) is amended—
(1) by striking out "(a)" before "No funds";
(2) by striking out "and reports, in a timely fashion" and all that follows in subsection (a) and inserting in lieu thereof a period and the following: "Each such operation shall be considered a significant anticipated intelligence activity for the purpose of section 501 of the National Security Act of 1947."; and
(3) by striking out subsection (b).
(b)(1) The National Security Act of 1947 (50 U.S.C. 401 et seq.) is amended by adding at the end thereof the following new title:

"TITLE V—ACCOUNTABILITY FOR INTELLIGENCE ACTIVITIES

"CONGRESSIONAL OVERSIGHT"

"SEC. 501. (a) To the extent consistent with all applicable authorities and duties, including those conferred by the Constitution upon the executive and legislative branches of the Government, and to the extent consistent with due regard for the protection from unauthorized disclosure of classified information and information relating to intelligence sources and methods, the Director of Central Intelligence and the heads of all departments, agencies, and other entities of the United States involved in intelligence activities shall—
"(1) keep the Select Committee on Intelligence of the Senate and the Permanent Select Committee on Intelligence of the House of Representatives (hereinafter in this section referred to as the 'intelligence committees') fully and currently informed of all intelligence activities which are the responsibility of, are engaged in by, or are carried out for or on behalf of, any department, agency, or entity of the United States, including any significant anticipated intelligence activity, except that (A) the foregoing provision shall not require approval of the intelligence committees as a condition precedent to the initiation of any such anticipated intelligence activity, and (B) if the President determines it is essential to limit prior notice to meet extraordinary circumstances affecting vital interests of the United States, such notice shall be limited to the chairman and ranking minority members of the intelligence committees, the Speaker and minority leader of the House of Representatives, and the majority and minority leaders of the Senate;
"(2) furnish any information or material concerning intelligence activities which is in the possession, custody, or control of any department, agency, or entity of the United States and which is requested by either of the intelligence committees in order to carry out its authorized responsibilities; and

"(3) report in a timely fashion to the intelligence committees any illegal intelligence activity or significant intelligence failure and any corrective action that has been taken or is planned to be taken in connection with such illegal activity or failure.

"(b) The President shall fully inform the intelligence committees in a timely fashion of intelligence operations in foreign countries, other than activities intended solely for obtaining necessary intelligence, for which prior notice was not given under subsection (a) and shall provide a statement of the reasons for not giving prior notice.

"(c) The President and the intelligence committees shall each establish such procedures as may be necessary to carry out the provisions of subsections (a) and (b).

"(d) the House of Representatives and the Senate, in consultation with the Director of Central Intelligence, shall each establish, by rule or resolution of such House, procedures to protect from unauthorized disclosure all classified information and all information relating to intelligence sources and methods furnished to the intelligence committees or to Members of the Congress under this section. In accordance with such procedures, each of the intelligence committees shall promptly call to the attention of its respective House, or to any appropriate committee or committees of its respective House, any matter relating to intelligence activities requiring the attention of such House or such committee or committees.

"(e) Nothing in this Act shall be construed as authority to withhold information from the intelligence committees on the grounds that providing the information to the intelligence committees would constitute the unauthorized disclosure of classified information or information relating to intelligence sources and methods."

INTELLIGENCE REQUIREMENTS FOR THE 1980's

Published by
National Strategy Information Center, Inc.
1730 Rhode Island Avenue, N.W., Washington, D.C. 20036
and
150 East 58th Street, New York, N.Y. 10155

Volume One
  Elements of Intelligence   First Edition—October, 1979
                                    Revised Edition—October, 1983

Volume Two
  Analysis and Estimates   June, 1980

Volume Three
  Counterintelligence   December, 1980

Volume Four
  Covert Action   September, 1981

Volume Five
  Clandestine Collection   October, 1982

Distributed by Transaction Books, New Brunswick (USA) and
London (UK).